A SHORT HISTORY OF CEYLON

The Colossal Buddha, Awkana.

A SHORT HISTORY
OF CEYLON

BY

HUMPHREY W. CODRINGTON

WITH A CHAPTER ON ARCHAEOLOGY BY

A. M. HOCART

WITH MAPS AND ILLUSTRATIONS

BOOKS FOR LIBRARIES PRESS
FREEPORT, NEW YORK

First Published 1926
Reprinted 1970

INTERNATIONAL STANDARD BOOK NUMBER:
0-8369-5596-X

LIBRARY OF CONGRESS CATALOG CARD NUMBER:
72-140353

PRINTED IN THE UNITED STATES OF AMERICA

CONTENTS

CONTENTS

LIST OF ILLUSTRATIONS

ix

MAPS AND PLANS

NOTE ON THE CHRONOLOGY OF CEYLON

THE first date absolutely fixed is that of the coronation of Sāhasa Malla in A.D. 1200. The reigns of previous kings as far back as Vijaya Bāhu I. can be dated correctly within a year ; the chronology between Sēna I. and the Chōla conquest at the beginning of the eleventh century is approximate. Before the accession of Sēna I. we have a few synchronisms to help us, and a certain number of dates given in the Buddhist era. These have been given in the text, but little reliance can be placed on them, except for the reign of Dēvānampiya Tissa. For the sake of convenience I have taken B.C. 247, as given in Geiger's *Mahā-vansa*, p. xxxiii, as the date of his first coronation. But this really is independent of any theory as to the date of Buddha's death, and depends on the synchronism with Asōka and ultimately on that with the contemporary Greek kings. There is no genuine trace of the employment of the Buddhist or of any era before the time of Parākrama Bāhu I. in the twelfth century ; in documents the reckoning is by regnal years, and the dates in the Buddhist era in the Pali and Sinhalese books after Dēvānampiya Tissa are due to computations by the various authors. Such calculations are made by adding up reigns, placed one after the other regardless of co-regencies and civil war. And the lengths of the reigns in the inscriptions do not always tally with the books ; thus we find no reign in the period between Mānavamma and Sēna I. agreeing

xiii

with that of an Abhā Salamevan, an inscription of whose forty-fifth year exists at Polonnaruwa. We have definite evidence of computation in the date 217 years 10 months and 10 days from the Conversion assigned to the foundation of Abhayagiri Vihāra by Vatta Gāmani. This obviously is based on the length of reigns, which with twenty-two years for Sēna and Guttika come to a total of 218 ; yet the prophecy as to Duttha Gāmani's accession when 136 years had passed from the Conversion presupposes that these two Tamils ruled for twelve years only (*Mhv.* xxvii. 6, 7). In the absence of any certainty for the period before the Chōla conquest I have merely noted the century, giving however, synchronisms where such occur. By this course confusion is not worse confounded by a new chronology as unreliable as the old. The real difficulty in adjustment lies in the period between the reigns of Kassapa I., fixed by a synchronism as about A.D. 527, and the accession of Sēna I., about A.D. 819. Aggabōdhi II. and Mānavamma were contemporaries of the Chalukya king Pulakēsin II., and it seems probable that the time between A.D. 527 and the accession of Mānavamma was shorter than it appears to be by adding up reigns ; it included a series of disputed successions. From the time of Vijaya Bāhu I. I have adopted the dates most recently fixed. In the list of Sovereigns before this reign, I have given for convenience the dates adopted by the *Mahāvansa* Editors.

LIST OF THE SOVEREIGNS OF CEYLON

Jēttha Tissa III.	-	-	-	A.D. 623		
Aggabōdhi III. (restored)	-	-	-	624		
Dāthōpatissa I.	-	-	-	640		
Kassapa II.	-	-	-	-	652	
Dappula I.	-	-	-	-	661	
Dāthōpatissa II.	-	-	-	664		
Aggabōdhi IV.	-	-	-	-	673	
Datta	-	-	-	-	689	
Unhanāgara Hatthadātha		-	-	691		
Mānavamma	-	-	-	-	691	
Aggabōdhi V.	-	-	-	-	726	
Kassapa III.	-	-	-	-	732	
Mahinda I.	-	-	-	-	738	
Aggabōdhi VI.	-	-	-	-	741	
Aggabōdhi VII.	-	-	-	781	Polonnaruwa.	
Mahinda II.	-	-	-	-	787	Anurādhapura.
Dappula II.	-	-	-	-	807	? A.D. 790.
Mahinda III.	-	-	-	-	812	
Aggabōdhi VIII.	-	-	-	816		
Dappula III.	-	-	-	-	827	
Aggabōdhi IX.	-	-	-	-	843	
Sēna I.	-	-	-	-	-	846	? A.D. 819/20. Polonnaruwa.
Sēna II.	-	-	-	-	-	866
Udaya I.	-	-	-	-	-	901
Kassapa IV.	-	-	-	-	912
Kassapa V.	-	-	-	-	929
Dappula IV.	-	-	-	-	939
Dappula V.	-	-	-	-	940	? c. A.D. 918/9.
Udaya II.	-	-	-	-	952
Sēna III.	-	-	-	-	-	955
Udaya III.	-	-	-	-	964	? c. A.D. 942/3.
Sēna IV.	-	-	-	-	-	972
Mahinda IV.	-	-	-	-	975
Sēna V.	-	-	-	-	-	991
Mahinda V.	-	-	-	-	1001	Deported c. A.D. 1017. Anurādhapura.

Kassapa or Vikrama Bāhu	-	-	1037	
Kitti	-	-	-	1049
Mahālāna Kitti	-	-	-	1049
Vikrama Pāndya	-	-	-	1052	Ruhuna.
Jagatipāla	-	-	-	1053
Parākrama	-	-	-	1057
Lokissara	-	-	-	1059
Vijaya Bāhu I.	-	-	-	1056-1111	Polonnaruwa.
Jaya Bāhu I.	-	-	-	1108-1145/6 + Polonnaruwa and Ruhuna.
(Vikrama Bāhu I.)	-	-	1111-1132	Polonnaruwa.
Gaja Bāhu II.	-	-	-	1131-1153	

Parākrama Bāhu I. -	- A.D. 1153-1186	
Vijaya Bāhu II. -	- 1186-1187	
Mahinda VI. - -	- 1187	
Nissanka Malla -	- 1187-1196	
Vīra Bāhu - -	- 1196	
Vikrama Bāhu II. -	- 1196	
Chōdaganga - -	- 1196-1197	
Līlāvatī (1) - -	- 1197-1200	
Sāhasa Malla - -	- 1200-1202	
Kalyānavatī - -	- 1202-1208	
Dharmāsōka - -	- 1208-1209	
Anikanga - -	- 1209	
Līlāvatī (2) - -	- 1209-1210	
Lokissara - -	- 1210-1211	
Līlāvatī (3) - -	- 1211-1212	
Parākrama Pāndya -	- 1212-1215	
Māgha - - -	- 1215-1236 +	
Vijaya Bāhu III. -	- c.1220-1224	Dambadeniya.
Parākrama Bāhu II. -	- 1234-1269	
Vijaya Bāhu IV. -	- 1267/8-1270	
Bhuvanaika Bāhu I. -	- 1271-1283	Dambadeniya and Yāpahu.
Interregnum - -	- 1283-1302	
Parākrama Bāhu III. -	c. 1302-1310 +	Polonnaruwa.
Bhuvanaika Bāhu II. -	? 1310-1325/6	Kurunēgala.
Parākrama Bāhu IV. -	1325/6-	
Bhuvanaika Bāhu III.		
Jaya (Vijaya) Bāhu		
Bhuvanaika Bāhu IV. -	1344/5-1353/4 +	Gampola.
Parākrama Bāhu V. -	1344/5-1359 +	Dedigama and Gampola.
Vikrama Bāhu III. -	- c. 1357-1374 +	Gampola.
Bhuvanaika Bāhu V. -	1372/3-1404/5 or 1406/7 +	Gampola.
Vīra Bāhu - -	- 1391/2-1396/7 +	Rayigama.
Vira Alakēsvara -	- c. 1397-1409	Rayigama.
(? Vijaya Bāhu VI.)		
Parākrama Bāhu Ēpā -	- 1409-? 1412	
Parākrama Bāhu VI. -	- 1412-1468	Kōttē.
Jaya Bāhu II. -	- 1468-1472/3	
Bhuvanaika Bāhu VĪ. -	1472/3-1480/1 +	
Parākrama Bāhu VII. -	1480/1-c. 1484	
Parākrama Bāhu VIII. -	c. 1484-1518	
Parākrama Bāhu IX. -	- 1509-1528 +	? Kelaniya.
Vijaya Bāhu VII. -	- 1509-1521	Kōttē
Bhuvanaika Bāhu VII. -	- 1521-1550	
Dharmapāla - -	- 1550-1597	

KINGS OF SITAWAKA

Māyādunnē - - - - - - -	1521-1581
Rājasinha I. - - - - - - -	1554-1593
Rājasūrya - - - - - - -	1593-1594

KINGS OF KANDY

Vimala Dharma Sūrya I. - - - - -	1590-1604
Senarat - - - - - - - -	1604-1635
Rājasinha II. - - - - - - -	c. 1629-1687
Vimala Dharma Sūrya II. - - -	1687-1707
Narēndra Sinha - - - - -	1707-1739
Vijaya Rājasinha - - - - - -	1739-1747
Kīrtisrī - - - - - - - -	1747-1780
Rājādhirājasinha - - - - - -	1780-1798
Srī Vikrama Rājasinha - - - - -	1798-1815

KINGS OF PORTUGAL AND CAPTAINS GENERAL

Philip I. 1580-1598.
Philip II. 1598-1621 :

Pedro Lopes de Sousa - - - - -	1594
D. Jeronimo de Azevedo - - - -	1594-1613
D. Francisco de Meneses - - - -	1613-1614
Manuel Mascarenhas Homem - - -	1614-1616
Nuno Alvares Pereira - - - - -	1616-1618
Constantino de Sa de Noronha - - -	1618-1622

Philip III. 1621-1640 :

Jorge de Albuquerque - - - - -	1622-1623
Constantino de Sa de Noronha - - -	1623-1630
D. Philippe Mascarenhas - - - -	1630-1631
D. Jorge de Almeida - - - - -	1631-1633
Diogo de Mello de Castro - - - -	1633-1635
D. Jorge de Almeida - - - - -	1635-1636
Diogo de Mello de Castro - - - -	1636-1638
D. Antonio Mascarenhas - - - -	1638-1640

John IV. of Braganza. 1640-1656 :

D. Philippe Mascarenhas - - - -	1640-1645
Manuel Mascarenhas Homem - - -	1645-1653
Francisco de Mello de Castro - - -	1653-1655
Antonio de Sousa Coutinho - - - -	1655-1656
Antonio de Amaral de Menezes - - -	1656-1658 Jaffna.

DUTCH GOVERNORS OF CEYLON

William J. Coster	1640
Jan Thyszoon Payart	1640-1646
Joan Maatzuyker	1646-1650
Jacob van Kittensteyn	1650-1653
Adriaan van der Meyden	1653-1660 and 1661-1663
Ryklof van Goens	1660-1661 and 1663
Jacob Hustaart	1663-1664
Ryklof van Goens	1664-1675
Ryklof van Goens, junr.	1675-1679
Laurens Pyl	1679-1692
Thomas van Rhee	1692-1697
Gerrit de Heere	1697-1702
Cornelis Jan Simons	1702-1706
Hendrik Becker	1706-1716
Isaac Augustin Rumpf	1716-1723
Johannes Hertenberg	1723-1726
Petrus Vuyst	1726-1729
Stephanus Versluys	1729-1732
Jacob Christiaan Pielat	1732-1734
Diederik van Domburg	1734-1736
Gustaaf Willem Baron van Imhoff	1736-1739
Willem Maurits Bruyninck	1739-1742
Daniel Overbeek	1742-1743
Julius V. S. van Gollenesse	1743-1751
Gerard Joan Vreeland	1751-1752
Johan Gideon Loten	1752-1757
Jan Schreuder	1757-1762
L. J. Baron van Eck	1762-1765
Iman Willem Falck	1765-1785
Willem J. van de Graaff	1785-1794
J. G. van Angelbeek	1794-1796

BRITISH GOVERNORS OF CEYLON

The Governor of Madras in Council	1796
The Hon. Frederick North	1798
Sir Thomas Maitland	1805
Sir Robert Brownrigg, Bart.	1812
The Hon. Sir Edward Paget	1822
Sir Edward Barnes	1824
Sir Robert W. Horton, Bart.	1831
J. A. S. Mackenzie	1837
Sir Colin Campbell	1841
Viscount Torrington	1847
Sir G. W. Anderson	1850

ABBREVIATIONS

A.I.C.	*Ancient Inscriptions of Ceylon*, E. Müller, 1883.
A.R.E.	*Annual Report of Epigraphy*, Southern Circle, Madras Government.
A.S.	*Archaeological Survey of Ceylon*, Ceylon Sessional Papers.
C.A.	*Ceylon Antiquary*.
De Q.	De Queyroz, *Conquista Temporal e Espiritual de Ceylão*, Colombo, 1916.
Dpv.	*Dipavamsa*, H. Oldenberg, 1879.
E.Z.	*Epigraphia Zeylanica*.
J.R.A.S.	*Journal of the Royal Asiatic Society*.
J.R.A.S., C.B.	*Journal of the Royal Asiatic Society*, Ceylon Branch.
Mhv.	*Mahāvansa*, L. C. Wijesinha, 1889 ; W. Geiger, 1912.
N.S.	*Nikāya Sangraha*, Colombo, 1908.
Puj.	*Pūjāvaliya*, Colombo, 1913.
Raj.	*Rājāvaliya*, Colombo, 1900.
Saddh.	*Saddharmaratnākaraya*, Colombo, 1912.

CHAPTER I

THE BEGINNINGS ; AND THE CONVERSION TO BUDDHISM

THE Island which is known by the name of Lankā, and to the western nations by that of Ceylon, is said to have been called in the time of the three previous Buddhas of the present age Ojadīpa, Varadīpa, and Mandadīpa respectively. To the Greeks and Romans it was Taprobane, in Pāli Tambapanni. This properly was the name of a district on the north-west coast, in ancient times the portion of the country best known to seafaring traders ; as in the case of India and of Asia itself the name of the part has been transferred to the whole. In the *Periplus* its older name is given as Taprobane and its modern as Palaisimundu. After the Sinhalese settlement it was styled in Sanskrit Sinhala-dvīpa, and in Pāli Sīhala-dīpa, a name which in process of time passed into Arabic as Serendib, or was known simply as Sinhala or Sīhala. This in the form Sinhalē still survives in common parlance as the name of the Kandyan districts, which last retained their independence, and is the origin of our ' Ceylon,' through the medium of Arabic and Portuguese ; in the Tamil it is represented by Ílam. In Sinhalese the letters S and H are often interchangeable, and the old language, untouched by Sanskrit and Tamil, is the Helu or Elu, names also derived from ' Sinhala.'

The Island in the mediaeval period, like Gaul in Caesar's time, ' divisa est in partes tres.'   These were Pihiti or Raja Rata or ' the King's Country,' Māyā Rata or ' the Country of the sub-king' (Mahayā, Māpā), and Ruhuna.   Of Māyā the boundaries were on the north the Deduru Oya, falling into the sea by Chilaw, and on the south the

FIG. 2.—The arrival of Sinhala.

Kaluganga, which separated it from Ruhuna.   This last named division extended all over the east and south of the Island, and was cut off from the rest by the Mahaweli-ganga, and, as we have seen, by the Kaluganga.   But these boundaries were theoretical only and liable to variation, and Māyā in the fourteenth century comprised much of the present Ratnapura and Kalutara Districts.

In early times we only hear of Ruhuna, then perhaps in

reality reaching the Kaluganga or even further north, and of Malaya, the ' Hill Country.' Later, we meet with the Northern, Southern, Eastern, and Western Countries ; these were not so named from their position in the Island, but from their situation relative to the capital Anurādhapura. The ' Southern Country,' which began in the south of the present North Central Province, developed into Māyā Rata and formed the appanage of the sub-king ; in the twelfth century it extended over the western part of Mātalē, the whole of the North-western Province, and the greater part of the Western and Sabaragamuwa Provinces. In the twelfth century Ruhuna itself was divided temporarily into two parts, Dolosdahas comprising the south and south-west and Atadahas the remainder. The north of the Island was the ' King's Country,' with its centre first at Anurādhapura and then at Polonnaruwa, and was under the immediate government of the king himself.

The earliest map of Ceylon which we possess is that of Ptolemy in the first century after Christ. In this the east coast with the mouth of the Ganges (Mahaweliganga) is plainly recognizable ; but the ' North Point ' is the modern Talaimannār, not far from which is the trading-town of Talakory, corresponding with the later Mahātittha or Mantota. The Hill Country or Malaya is shown under this name, and the two chief cities were the ' Royal City,' Anurogrammon or Anurādhapura, and the ' Metropolis ' Maagrammon (Sanskrit, Mahāgrāma) on the Mahaweli-ganga : this last has been identified with Mahiyangana, the modern Alutnuwara, but may have been lower down stream and not far from Māgam-tota by Polonnaruwa. The termination ' grammon,' ' village,' instead of ' pura,' ' city,' is of interest. Before Ptolemy's time the west coast of Ceylon was supposed to extend almost as far as

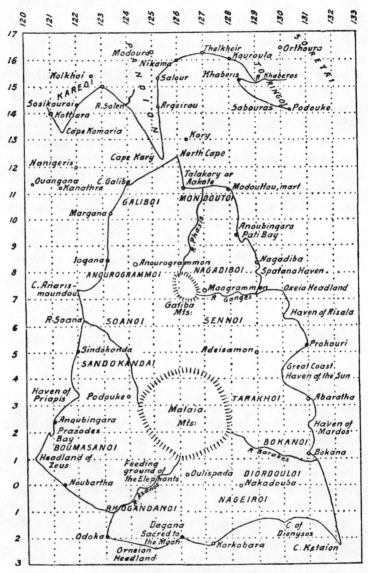

PTOLEMY'S TAPROBANE

Map I.

Africa. An explanation of this may be found in the fact that the east coast of that continent in the neighbourhood of Zanzibar was known to the Greeks as Azania, and that a river on the west coast of Ceylon according to Ptolemy was the Azanos.

Megasthenes, the Greek ambassador to the court of Chandragupta (B.C. 321-297), knew of Ceylon but vaguely ; he calls its people Palaeogoni. Pliny records that in the reign of Claudius (A.D. 41-54), a freedman of Annius Plocamus, who had rented the customs of the Red Sea, while sailing round Arabia was caught by the north winds and driven past the coast of Carmania (Mekran) to Ceylon, where he made land on the fifteenth day at the port of Hippuros, presumably on the south-west coast of the Island. He was taken to the ' king,' who entertained him for six months, and afterwards sent an embassy to Rome. The port is said to have faced the south, and to have been close to the chief city Palaesimundus on the river of the same name, which had three mouths. This stream as well as another, the Cydara, which ran northwards towards India, were reported to flow out of a vast lake, Megisba, in the interior. The nearest point of India was the Coliac headland, Ptolemy's Cory, or Rāmēsvaram, four days' sail away. The *Periplus* apparently derives its name for the Island, Palaesimundu, from this account.

The legendary history of Ceylon begins with the *Rāmā-yana*, the epic poem which recounts the ravishing of Sītā by the demon king of Lankā, Rāvana, and her recovery by her husband Rāma with the aid of the monkey chief Hanumanta. But, though a few names in the Island refer to the legend, such as Nuwara Eliya, ' the glade of (Rāvana's) city,' Sītā Eliya, ' Sītā's glade,' and Sītāwaka, the epic itself seems to have found but a small place in the folklore of the Sinhalese.

To them of much greater interest were the visits of Buddha to Ceylon. Of these the first was the visit to Mahiyangana, when, after expelling the Yakkhas or demon inhabitants of the country, he gave to Saman a lock of his hair, which that god enshrined in a sapphire casket. The second visit was to Nāgadīpa (the Jaffna Peninsula), when Buddha settled a dispute between the Nāga princes, Mahōdara and Chulōdara, concerning a gem-set throne. The third visit was to Kelaniya, where Buddha stayed at the site of the later dāgaba : thence he went to Samanta-kūta or Adam's Peak, on which he set the imprint of his foot, to Dīghavāpi in the present Eastern Province, and to Anurādhapura, where he sanctified by his presence various sites, including those of the Bo-tree and of the Ruwanweli Dāgaba.[1] Anurādhapura itself according to the legend had also been hallowed by the visits of the three previous Buddhas of the present age, in whose times it was called Abhayapura, Vaddhamāna, and Visālanagara. There is no historical foundation for the visits of Gautama Buddha or of his three predecessors. The legendary inhabitants of the country were the Yakkhas, the Nāgas and the Dēvas, and under these names possibly a kernel of fact may be concealed.

The traditional first king of Ceylon is Vijaya. His grandmother, Suppadēvī, according to the legend was the daughter of the king of Vanga (Bengal) by a princess of Kalinga (Orissa). She ran away from home and in the country of Lāla or Lāda, the modern Gujarat, mated with a lion (sinha) ; whence the names of her children and ultimately that of Sinhala, the designation of Ceylon and of the Sinhalese. At the age of sixteen her son Sinhabāhu carried off his mother and his twin sister to the haunts of

---

[1] Dāgaba.   A relic shrine, a solid hemispherical monument sur-mounted by a spire.

men ; the lion in his search for his family ravaged the country, and for the sake of the reward offered by the king of Vanga was slain by his own son. The king dying at the time, Sinhabāhu was elected as his successor, but abandoned Vanga and built the city of Sinhapura in his native country Lāda. His son Prince Vijaya and his boon companions committed such outrages in his father's capital that the king was compelled by popular clamour to drive them forth. They set sail and, touching at Suppāraka, a famous port on the west coast of India (Sopara, north of Bombay), ultimately arrived at Tambapanni. Here they found the country inhabited by Yakkhas or demons, and one of them Kuvēni, entrapped Vijaya's followers, but was compelled by the prince to release them. She then became Vijaya's mistress, and assisted him to exterminate her fellow-demons, whose chief seats are given as Sirivatthu and Lankāpura. These were identified later with the hills Loggala and Laggala, though it is clear from the narrative that Sirivatthu was quite close to Vijaya's landing place, as he heard the noise of the wedding festivities, of which he took advantage to attack the Yakkhas. Vijaya now settled at Tambapanni, a port on the south of the river, perhaps the Malwatu Oya, and his followers formed various villages in the neighbouring country : these were Anurādhapura on the banks of the Malwatu Oya ; Upatissa, seven or eight miles further north ; Uruvēla, a seaport to the west of Anurādhapura, perhaps at Marichchikatti ; Ujjēni and Vijita. His followers now wished Vijaya to assume the crown, and dispatched an embassy in search of a queen to the Pāndyan king at Madura. The princess and her retinue landed at Mahātittha (Mantota) ; she espoused Vijaya and her women his companions, while the discarded Kuvēni with her two children wandered to Lankāpura, and was

slain by her enraged kinsfolk. The children fled to
Adam's Peak and became the ancestors of the Pulindas
(hill-men or Veddas).

Such is the received story in Ceylon. But it is to be
noted that there is no mention of the Kuvēni legend in
the oldest chronicle, the *Dīpavansa*. Another and Indian
version of the colonization of Ceylon relates the story of
the princess and the lion; but here the son, though re-
warded for slaying the wild beast, is banished for his
parricide and retires to the Island of Gems (Ratnadvīpa).
Merchants coming to the country in search of precious
stones, the lion's son kills their chief and detains his family.
In course of time, his descendants becoming numerous, a
king is elected and a state established, when the country
is called Sinhala from the name of the original founder.
A third account tells how demon women dwelt in an iron
city in Ratnadvīpa, and how they allured mariners ashore.
Sinhala the son of King Sinha in India comes with 500
merchants to the country in search of precious stones.
They marry the demon women. Sinhala, however, finds
out their true nature, and by means of a flying horse
carries off his companions. The women pursue and
induce them to return. But Sinhala is obdurate. His
wife, the queen of the demon women, follows him to India,
and being rejected by him is taken under his father's
protection. She summons her people and kills all in the
palace. Sinhala is then elected king in his father's place,
invades the Island of Gems, rescues his men, and bringing
colonists establishes the kingdom of Sinhala. This tale
is founded upon the ' Birth Story of the Cloud Horse '
(Valāhaka Jātaka). In that legend the demon city
Sirīsavatthu in Ceylon is peopled by she-demons, who
catch shipwrecked sailors and scour the coast between
Kalyāni (Kelaniya) and the Island Nāgadīpa. Five

hundred merchants are wrecked and are entertained by the demons. The chief merchant finds that their hosts are demons, and escapes with 250 of his men by means of a flying horse, who is the Buddha in a previous existence. The remainder are devoured by the demons. It is evident that the story of Vijaya is a combination of various fairy tales.

Shortly before his death, Vijaya, who was without an heir, sent a letter to Sinhapura, asking that his brother Sumitta should be sent to succeed him. Sumitta, however, was now king in his father's place, and dispatched his youngest son, Panduvāsa, who in due course arrived in Ceylon and reigned at Vijitapura. Of this king a late legend tells how the perjury of which Vijaya had been guilty in repudiating Kuvēni was visited on his nephew, and how the god Sakra, to whom Lankā had been entrusted by Buddha, obtained his cure. Isvara instructed by Sakra called upon Rahu, who, turning himself into a boar, ravaged the garden of Mala Raja. The last named summoned his men to surround the garden and beat the jungle ; but the boar escaped, and, pursued by Mala Raja, leaped into the sea at Tuticorin, and swam, still pursued, across to Ūrātota (' Boar landing-place,' or Kayts) in Ceylon. When Rahu had enticed Mala Raja into the heart of the country he disappeared, leaving in his place a rock at which Mala Raja stood gazing in wonderment. Sakra now appeared and bade him cure the king, which he did. Panduvāsa married the daughter of the Sākya Pandu, the first cousin of Buddha, who was followed to Ceylon by her brothers. To them also is attributed the foundation of Anurādhapura, Uruvēla, Vijitapura, as well as of Dīghāyu and Rohana, identified later with Māgama in Hambantota District. Panduvāsa was succeeded by his son Abhaya, and he in turn after an interregnum of seventeen years by his nephew Pandukābhaya, who made Anurādhapura his capital. Here he constructed the Abhaya tank, now called Basavakkulam, and also established two Yakkha princes, one of whom sat on a throne of equal eminence with the king's. From this it is clear that the Yakkha or aboriginal population was not treated as a conquered race ; Vijaya's followers espoused Pāndyan women, and it seems probable that in course of time their descendants married with the people of the country, on whom they imposed their Āryan language. Further dilution of the original Āryan blood undoubtedly has taken place in later ages, with the result that, though the Sinhalese language is of North Indian origin, the social system is that of the south. In the twelfth year of his reign Pandukābhaya 'fixed the boundaries of the villages in all parts of Lankā.' He was succeeded by his son Mutasiva.

It is obvious that many of these events assigned to the early reigns are purely mythical. Two points call for comment. In the first place, if there is any truth in the account of Vijaya's ancestry at all, it is difficult to admit the probability of any connection between petty kings of Bengal and Gujarat on opposite sides of the Indian continent : the evidence all points to Vijaya having come from the western coast, and it seems likely that the tale of his mixed ancestry is due to the fact that there were two streams of immigration, one from the western and the other from the eastern side of India. The story of the double origin of such places as Anurādhapura, indicating two incompatible traditions, points this way, and without some such theory it is difficult to account for the early settlements at Māgama and its neighbourhood on the south and south-east coasts. It is possible and even probable that Vijaya (' the Conqueror ') himself is a composite character combining in his person the two conquests. In the second place, there is manifest a desire to connect the early history of Ceylon with that of Buddha. Vijaya is made to land at Tambapanni on the very day of Buddha's death. To give effect to this, the reigns of Vijaya and his four successors are extended over the impossibly long period of 236 years, of which 130 have to be divided between Pandukābhaya and his son Mutasiva. The latter's successor, as we shall see, came to the throne about B.C. 247, and it will be safe to place the arrival of Vijaya in the last years of the fifth century before Christ.

Though history really commences with the reign of Dēvānampiya Tissa (Devanapē Tissa, B.C. 247-207) and the conversion of Ceylon to the Buddhist faith, it must be remembered that many events recorded in the chronicles are still of a fictitious nature. Tissa was the second son of Mutasiva. It is stated in the *Mahāvansa* that on the day of his coronation many wonderful treasures miraculously appeared and that the king resolved to present them to the Indian Emperor Dharmāsōka, with whom he had been long united by ties of friendship. Accordingly an embassy was dispatched to Pātaliputra (Patna). The emperor in return sent back the ambassadors with all the requisites for a coronation, and with instructions to celebrate the inauguration of the Sinhalese king, whom at the same time he invited to embrace Buddhism. On their return to Ceylon the king was solemnly crowned a second time.

Dharmāsōka, or Asōka, as he is commonly called (B.C. 268-231),[1] was the grandson of Chandragupta, the founder of the Maurya empire and the contemporary of Alexander the Great. His remorse at the miseries caused by him in the conquest of Kalinga drove him to seek refuge in

[1] B.C. 274-237 according to the *Cambridge History of India*.

Buddhism. He was ruler of most of India, and used his power for the extension of his new faith, causing missions to be sent to various countries, even to the Greek kingdoms in Asia and Africa.

The question may be asked why Dēvānampiya Tissa should have sought confirmation of his sovereignty from Asōka. He may have done so on account of the commanding position of Asōka in India, though his imperial authority did not extend to the southernmost kingdoms of the peninsula. Or, again, it may have been due to family connections. Asōka was the head of the Maurya clan, and later on in Ceylon we find the Moriyas as a branch of the royal family. The *Mahāvansa* relates that the Sākya Pandu, the father-in-law of Panduvāsa, owing to war left his home and retired beyond the Ganges. Later works state that the new city then founded was called Moriya, and that from its ruling family, the Sākyas, known throughout India as Moriyas, sprang Chandragupta ; that Asōka himself married a Sākya princess and that her eight brothers accompanied the Bo-tree to Ceylon. Of these eight, the two elder, Bōdhigupta and Sumitta, received the offices of Lak Maha Lē (Chief Scribe of Ceylon) and Jaya Maha Lē (Chief Scribe of the victorious Bo-tree), and from them descended the Mehenavara and Ganavesi branches of the Sinhalese royal family ; another, who was given the Moriya district in the Island, is stated to have belonged to the ' Sākya race called Moriya.' As Pandu-kābhaya was the son of a Sākya prince, a nephew of Panduvāsa's queen, it follows that Dēvānampiya Tissa, his grandson, also was a Sākya. If there is any truth in this account Dēvanampiya Tissa was related to Asōka. The identification of Panduvāsa's brothers-in-law and of the Moriyas with the Sākyas doubtless was due to the desire to connect the royal family of Ceylon and the Buddhist Constantine with the race of Buddha himself.

As we have seen, one of the principal events of Asōka's reign was the dispatch of missionaries to propagate the Buddhist faith. Among these was his own son the Elder Mahinda, who arrived in Ceylon in the year of Dēvānampiya Tissa's second coronation, and met the king while hunting at the hill afterwards known as Mihintalē, eight miles from Anurādhapura. The sovereign, whose attention already had been drawn to Buddhism by Asōka, lost no time in embracing the new religion, and with him large numbers of his subjects. What his religion had been is not known : from the fact that Pandukābhaya built a temple for a Nighantha it may be supposed that it was Jainism, but Hindu ascetics also are mentioned. Dēvānampiya Tissa now dedicated to the priesthood the Nandana and Mahāmēgha royal pleasure gardens, situated to the south of the city, and built there the famous Mahā Vihāra,[1] for many centuries the centre of Ceylon orthodoxy. This event took place when eighteen years had passed since Asōka's coronation, and 236 years since the death of Buddha, or, reckoning this as having occurred about B.C. 483, in B.C. 247. The king's next work of piety was the construction of the Vihāra on Mihintalē, on which hill the ' bed ' of Mahinda still is to be seen : this was followed by the enshrining of the right collar-bone of Buddha, obtained from the god Sakra, in the Thūpārāma, the first of the dāgabas erected in Anurādhapura. The alms-bowl of Buddha was given at the same time by Asōka and kept in the royal palace.

The desire of the Princess Anulā with her attendants to enter the Second Order, or that of nuns, led to an embassy to the Court of Asōka with a request for the dispatch of

Vihāra. A residence of Buddhist monks ; a Buddhist temple.

Mahinda's sister Sanghamittā, a member of that Order, with the right branch of the Bo-tree, under which Gautama had attained Buddhahood. The branch, which miraculously severed itself from the parent tree, was conveyed down the Ganges together with Sanghamittā, and arrived in Ceylon at the port of Jambukōla (Sambilturai in the Jaffna peninsula), where it was received with all honour by Dēvānampiya Tissa. Conveyed to Anurādhapura it was planted in the Mahāmēgha garden, where it still exists, the oldest authenticated tree in the world.

Other religious buildings erected by Dēvānampiya Tissa were the Mahiyangana Dāgaba, in which Buddha's collar-bone was enshrined by the king's younger brother, and the Isurumuniya and Vessagiri Vihāras at the capital. He also constructed the Tisā-vewa tank at Anurādhapura. He died after a reign of forty years ; Mahinda survived his royal convert until the eighth year of his successor Uttiya.

We are confronted again with a chronological difficulty. Dēvānampiya Tissa was succeeded by four of his brothers, to each of whom is assigned a reign of ten years, a suspiciously symmetrical figure. The reigns of the last two are divided by the rule of two Tamils, Sēna and Guttika, the first of many such intruders, lasting for twelve or twenty-two years. The youngest of the brothers, Asēla, was succeeded by a Tamil, Ēlāra, who reigned forty-four years. We thus find that the reigns of five brothers and of the two Tamils lasted 92 or 102 years, an impossible figure, the more so as Kākavanna Tissa of Māgama, the contemporary of Ēlāra, was the great-grandson of Mahānāga, another brother of Dēvānampiya Tissa.

In this chapter we have seen the arrival of the immigrants from the north, the gradual establishment of the Sinhalese monarchy, and, most important event of all, the conversion of the country to Buddhism. The profession of this faith in later times has sharply separated Ceylon from her immediate neighbours and has had an abiding influence on the national character. Her renown as the centre of orthodoxy and of Pāli literature, however, is due to Buddhaghōsa and his school in the fifth century.

As the Island in the course of its history was in constant communication, peaceful or otherwise, with the mainland, the principal political divisions of South India for the sake of convenience are noted here. The chief Tamil-speaking kingdoms were : (1) the Pāndyan, comprising the greater part of the Madura and Tinnevelly Districts, with its capital first at Kolkai and later at Madura ; (2) the Chōla, extending along the Coromandel Coast northwards as far as the Penner River, the chief city at one time being Uraiyūr or Old Trichinopoly : and (3) the Chēra or Kērala on the south-west coast, where the language gradually developed into Malayālam ; with this was united (4) the once independent Kongu country, stretching over Coimbatore and part of Salem Districts. The royal emblems were a pair of fishes for the Pāndyans, a seated tiger for the Chōlas, and a bow for the Chēras. That of the later Sinhalese kings was a lion.

AUTHORITIES FOR CHAPTER I

For implements attributed to the Palaeolithic and Neolithic ages see John Pole, *Ceylon Stone Implements*, Calcutta, 1913. For the old names of Ceylon, see *Dpv.* i. 73 ; ix. 20 ; xvii. 5, 6 ; and *Mhv.* xv. 59, 92, 127 ; *Periplus*, ed. W. H. Schoff, 1912. The identity of the ' Southern Country ' is discussed in ' Notes on Ceylon Topography,' *J.R.A.S., C.B.,* xxix. No. 75, p. 62. For Ptolemy see *Ancient India*, by J. W. M'Crindle, 1885.

Hippuros usually is identified with Kudiraimalai, ' Horse

hill,' a promontory to the north of Puttalam. But it has not been shown why this one name should have been translated into Greek, and the wind would have driven the ships to the part of Ceylon indicated in the text.

The visits of the four Buddhas are recorded at some length in *Dpv*. ii. 66-69; xv. 25, 37, 47, 48, 54, 59; xvii. 30; and *Mhv*. i. 20-84. As to the Vijayan conquest the view that there were two streams of immigration is that of the *Cambridge History of India*, p. 606. For Tambapanni see *De Q.*, p. 4. Parker's view that it was in the south of Ceylon is based on a mistranslation of *Dpv*. ix. 33, the ' south ' referring to the river. But De Q. mentions a tradition that Vijaya landed near the Walawē in addition to legends as to two other sites.

The two stories of Sinhala are given in *Si-yu-ki*, by Hiuen Tsiang, translated by S. Beal in *Buddhist Records of the Western World*. Sirīsavatthu of the Jātaka is called Tammenna in the Sinhalese version. These legends are given in English in ' Prehistoric Ceylon,' by A. M. Gunasekera (*Ceylon National Review*, 1906, pp. 149 ff.). Sirīsavatthu presumably is the Sirivatthu of the Mahāvansa ; the Tammenna of the Sinhalese version is the place of the name in the neighbourhood of Puttalam, the traditional landing place of Vijaya. It may be noted that in Sanskrit ' sinhala ' has the meaning of ' bark,' ' Cassia bark ' (Cinnamomum cassia).

For Dēvānampiya Tissa, see *Dpv.*, *Mhv.*, and *Puj*. The tentative suggestion that the king's embassy to Asōka was due to relationship has been made by the Archaeological Commissioner, Mr. A. M. Hocart ; the details have been elaborated independently. For the account of the Sākyas and their identity with the Mauryas see *Mhv. Tīkā*, pp. 119 ff., and *Saddh*. pp. 265, 295, 296, and 325.

CHAPTER II

DUTTHA GĀMANI TO KASSAPA OF SIGIRIYA

THIRD CENTURY B.C.–SIXTH CENTURY A.D.

ÉLĀRA, or as he is called in Sinhalese Elāla, was a Tamil from the Chōla country, of which Tanjore was the capital in mediaeval times : he invaded Ceylon and put Asēla to death. Though a Hindu, his justice commanded the respect of his Sinhalese subjects. Concerning this the *Mahāvansa* relates that the king had a bell with a rope attached at the head of his bed, so that all who sought redress might ring it. Among other instances of the royal justice the chronicle tells how a calf was killed unintentionally by the chariot wheel of the king's son, and how, on the mother cow ringing the bell, the father had the prince's head struck off by the same wheel. The story is also told in Tamil literature of the Chōla king Manu.

At this period there were branches of the royal family established at Kelaniya and at Māgama in the present Hambantota District. The queen of Dēvānampiya Tissa tried to poison her brother-in-law, the sub-king Mahānāga, who thereupon fled towards Ruhuna. On the way his wife gave birth to a son, Tissa, at the Yatthāla Vihāra, whence, proceeding to Ruhuna, he established himself at Māgama. The site of Tissa's birthplace usually is identified with a temple near Galle, but it is clear from the narrative that it was not in Ruhuna : possibly it was the vihāra of the same name in Kēgalla District.

Tissa is said in the *Pūjāvaliya* to have built the Kelani Dāgaba : he, his son Gōthābhaya, and his grandson Kākavanna Tissa (Kāvan Tissa, 'Crow-colour Tissa '), succeeded to the government of the principality or

c.c.   B

kingdom of Māgama ; the last named ruler's wife was the
daughter of Tissa, king of Kelaniya. The queen of this
king Tissa had carried on an intrigue with her brother-in-
law, who on being detected fled and corresponded with
her by a messenger disguised as a priest. The man
attached himself to the attendants of the chief priest
who was visiting the palace, and catching the eye of the
queen dropped his master's letter. Unfortunately the
palm-leaf missive made a noise in falling ; the correspondence was detected, and the king in his fury slew not
only the messenger but the chief priest, whose complicity
he suspected. Thereupon the sea, which according to
the *Rājāvaliya* was then about seven gaus (some fifteen
miles) from Kelaniya, overwhelmed the land, submerging
many towns and villages. To put an end to this the king
placed his daughter Dēvī in a golden vessel and launched
it into the sea : she was carried southwards and cast
ashore near a temple (vihāra), when she became the queen
consort of Kākavanna Tissa under the name of Vihāra
Dēvī. Their sons were Gāmani Abhaya, the future hero,
and Tissa.

Gāmani Abhaya at an early age showed signs of an
adventurous disposition, and in particular resented the
confined limits of his father's kingdom, which was bounded
by the Mahaweliganga, on the other bank of which the
Tamils ruled. The young prince surrounded himself with
a chosen band of companions, finally asked permission of
his father to fight the Tamils, and, being refused, fled in
anger to the hills, thus earning by his conduct the surname
of ' Duttha,' ' bad.' On the death of his father, Duttha
Gāmani (Dutu Gemunu), as we must now call him,
succeeded to the kingdom, though not without an armed
struggle with his brother, with whom he was finally
reconciled.

FIG. 3.—A Battle.

Duttha Gāmani was now free to open his campaign against Ēlāra. Advancing through the hills on his famous state elephant Kandula (Kadol), he commenced operations at Mahiyangana, and gradually fought his way down the Mahaweliganga river. The Tamils at last threw themselves into Vijitapura, the siege of which took four months. This town usually is identified with the place now called by this name near Kalāvewa : but, as it was garrisoned by those Tamils ' who had escaped the slaughter along the bank of the river,' it seems more probable that it was in the neighbourhood of the later Polonnaruwa, a suburb of which in the twelfth century still went by the name of Vijita. This place undoubtedly is better situated than Kalāvewa for the next operation, the reduction of Girilaka, if this be Giritalē. Duttha Gāmani then advanced to the Kasa mountain or Kahagala, fifteen miles south-west of Anurādhapura, where he fortified himself and awaited the onset of Ēlāra. In the battle which ensued Ēlāra fled towards the capital ; but he was pursued by Duttha Gāmani and slain by him in single combat close to the southern gate of the city. His body was burnt with royal honours, and such was the respect in which he was held that succeeding kings of Ceylon silenced their musical instruments when passing his tomb in procession. The so-called Elāla Sohona or Tomb of Elāla at Anurādhapura does not mark his burial-place, but is the Dakkhina Thūpa or Southern Dāgaba.

Duttha Gāmani (second or first century B.C.), having disposed of reinforcements which arrived from India under Ēlāra's nephew, was now sole monarch of Lankā, and kept the feast of his coronation. On the seventh day thereafter he celebrated an aquatic festival at Tisā-vewa. At its conclusion he found that he was unable to take up his spear, into which a relic had been inserted, from the ground, and, considering this a miracle, began the building of the Mirisveti Dāgaba on that spot, in penance for his failure to share with the priesthood a ripe chilly-pod (*miris*). He also constructed the Brazen Palace, so called from its tiles being of brass : this also is attributed to Dēvānampiya Tissa. His chief work of piety, however, was the great Ruwanweli Dāgaba or Mahā Thūpa, erected upon the site where Buddha had stayed on his third visit to Ceylon. The huge mass was still unfinished and lacking the spire when Duttha Gāmani fell sick. His younger brother, Saddhā Tissa, having covered the dāgaba with white cloth and crowned it with a spire of bamboo, the king was brought out and died, his eyes fixed on his masterpiece. He had reigned twenty-four years. Duttha Gāmani, as seen by later generations, too well acquainted with Dravidian conquerors, became the heroic figure of Sinhalese history, the expeller of the foreigner and the restorer of the national religion.

The new king, Saddhā Tissa, rebuilt the Brazen Palace, which had been burnt, and formed the Padi tank or Padawiya in the North Central Province. To him is ascribed the inscription by the drip-line over the great cave temple of Dambulla, though tradition attributes the construction of this shrine to Vatta Gāmani.

After three of Saddhā Tissa's sons had ruled, a fourth, by name Vatta Gāmani (Valagam Abha, first century B.C.) came to the throne, but was expelled by Tamil invaders in the fifth month of his reign, and concealed himself in the hill country. Five Tamils, apparently Pāndyans, maintained their hold of the capital for fourteen years : the last was slain by Vatta Gāmani, who thus regained his sovereignty. Now the king on his flight from Anurādhapura had been mocked by a Jain ascetic of the establishment founded by Pandukābhaya, and had then resolved, if he were successful, to build a vihāra on the spot. This he now proceeded to carry out, and built the great Abhayagiri Dāgaba, said to have been completed in the 218th

year from the foundation of the Mahā Vihāra : this
structure is not the one commonly called by the name,
but that now styled the Jētavanārāma. North of Ruwanweli Dāgaba the king constructed the Silāsōbbhakandaka
Dāgaba, the modern Lankārāma ; and his soldier Uttiya
the Dakkhina or ' Southern ' Vihāra, now known as
' Elāla's Tomb.'

In this reign we hear of the first dissension in the priest-
hood, the Abhayagiri fraternity separating itself from the
Mahā Vihāra under the name of the Dharmaruchi sect.
It is stated that at the same period and on account of

FIG. 4.—Early Coin.

false doctrine the Buddhist scriptures (*Tripitaka*) and
their commentaries, hitherto handed down by word of
mouth, were recorded in books. The traditional site of
the convocation assembled for this purpose is Aluvihārē,
near Mātalē.

Among the successors of Vatta Gāmani appears the
infamous queen Anulā. She first poisoned two husbands,
then ruled by means of four paramours in succession, and
having rid herself of them by poison finally governed
openly alone, but was speedily supplanted by Kutakanna
Tissa (about the beginning of the Christian era). This
king built a wall seven cubits high round Anurādhapura.
His grandson Āmanda Gāmani was the founder of the

well-known Ridī Vihāra in Kurunēgala District, a temple
which derives its name from the silver miraculously discovered at this place for the purpose of constructing the
Ruwanweli Dāgaba. Ila Nāga (first century A.D.) built the
great dāgaba at Tissamahārāma,
then known as the Nāga Mahā
Vihāra. Vasabha, his fourth successor, raised in height Kutakanna
Tissa's wall round the capital ; if
we are to believe the later chronicle it had a circumference of

Fig. 5.—Gold Indo-Roman
Coin.

sixteen gaus, or over thirty-five miles. Vasabha did
much for irrigation, constructing eleven tanks ; the
Elahera channel, which took water to Kawdulu-vewa, is
mentioned in his reign.

The monotony of piety and murder is broken by
Gāmani, nicknamed Gaja Bāhu or ' elephant arm ' (second
century A.D.). A king of little account in the older
chronicle, he has attained a certain fame in popular legend.
According to the mediaeval account, in the time of his
father, 12,000 men had been sent to work at Kāvēri on
the Coromandel coast ; in the late *Rājāvaliya* this has
developed into an invasion by the Chōla king. Gaja
Bāhu, while walking in the city one night, heard a widow
weeping because her children had been carried off. The
king, who was unaware of what had happened in his
father's time, assembled his army, but resolved to accom-
plish his purpose unaided in person. The *Rājāvaliya*
relates the story thus :

' Taking the giant Nīla with him he went and struck the
sea with an iron mace, divided the waters in twain, and
going quietly on arrived at the Soli capital, struck terror
into the king of Soli, and seated himself on the throne like
King Sak ; whilst the giant Nīla seized the elephants

in the city and killed them by striking one against another.

'The ministers informed the king of Soli of the devastation of the city thus being made. Thereupon he inquired of Gajabā, " Is the Sinhalese host come to destroy this city ? " Gajabā replied, " I have a little boy who accompanied me ; there is no army," and caused the giant Nīla to be brought and made to stand by his side. Thereupon the king of Soli asked, " Why has your Majesty come along without an army ? " Gajabā replied, " I have come to take back the 12,000 persons whom your royal father brought here as prisoners in the time of my father." To this the king of Soli saying, " A king of our family it was who, in time past, went to the city of the gods and gained victory in the war with the Asuras," refused to send for and deliver the men. Then Gajabā grew wroth and said, " Forthwith restore my 12,000 people, giving 12,000 more besides them ; else will I destroy this city and reduce it to ashes." Having said this, he squeezed out water from sand and showed it ; squeezed water from his iron mace and showed that. Having in this way intimidated the king of Soli he received the original number supplemented by an equal number of men as interest, making 24,000 persons in all. He also took away the jewelled anklets of the goddess Pattini, and the insignia of the gods of the four dēvāla, and also the bowl-relic which had been carried off in the time of king Valagambā ; and admonishing the king not to act thus in future, departed.'

The story continues that the 24,000 were distributed by the king in different districts, thus accounting for such names as Sārasiyapattuwa, ' the 400 pattu,' and the like. Similar names of districts, however, occur in India. The tradition as to the goddess Pattini may have some foun-

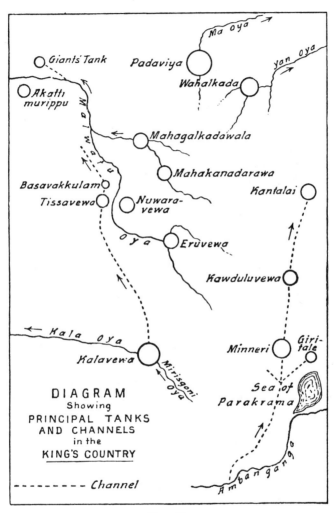

Ma oya

Yan oya

Giants' Tank

Padaviya

Wahalkada

Akatti murippu

Mahagalkadawala

Mahakanadarawa

Basavakkulam

Kantalai

Tissavewa

Nuwara-vewa

Eruvewa

Kawduluvewa

Kala oya

Minneri

Giri-tale

Kalavewa

Mirisgoni oya

Sea of Parakrama

DIAGRAM
Showing
PRINCIPAL TANKS
AND CHANNELS
in the
KING'S COUNTRY

Ambanganga

- - - - - - - Channel

MAP II.

dation in fact, as in ancient Tamil literature Gaja Bāhu of Lankā attended the consecration of the Pattini temple at Vanji by the Chēra king Senguttavan. To this king's maternal grandfather, the Chōla Karikāla, is attributed the construction of embankments along the Kāvēri river.

Vōhārika Tissa (third century A.D.), so called from his knowledge of law and from having set judicial business free from maiming, or perhaps torture, suppressed the Vaitulya heresy, a Mahāyāna or northern form of Buddhism which had appeared at Abhayagiri. He is said to have come to the throne when 752 years had passed since the death of Buddha.

Thirty-three years later three members of the Lambakanna (Lemeni, ' having ears with long lobes ') branch of the royal family conspired against the reigning King Vijaya, slew him, and set the eldest, Sanghatissa, on the throne. He was succeeded by the second, Siri Sanghabōdhi (Siri Sangabo, third or early fourth century A.D.), who has become a saintly figure in popular story. Of him it is related that in a severe drought he threw himself on the ground before the Ruwanweli Dāgaba, and resolved not to rise therefrom until rain should have fallen sufficient to lift him from the earth. Rain immediately fell, but, as the king who was not floating on the water still refused to rise, his household officers stopped up the drains and enabled him to fulfil his vow. Again, on the occasion of an epidemic, attributed to a red-eyed demon, the king compelled the monster to appear and offered himself in satisfaction of his hunger. This offer was politely refused, and instead ' bali ' offerings were instituted throughout Ceylon. The third Lambakanna, Gōthakābhaya (Golu Abā), rebelled against him, and Siri Sanghabōdhi, abhorring the idea of being the cause of death to others, fled southwards from the capital. The usurper offered a reward for his head. A traveller happened to meet the king, whom he did not recognize, and pressed his own food and drink upon him. The king ate, and in order to reward the man

FIG. 6.—Persian Cross, Anurādhapura.

proclaimed his identity, and bade him take his head. On his refusal Siri Sanghabōdhi severed his own head, which was duly taken to Gōthakābhaya. The story has grown in course of time, later versions telling how the usurper refused to believe that it was his rival's head, and how the head sprang up thrice by the power of the gods saying,

' I am King Siri Sangabo.'' Gōthakābhaya made amends
by erecting a shrine over the late king's burial-place at
Attanagalla.

In Gōthakābhaya's fourth year some of the Abhayagiri
monks adopted the Vaitulya heresy once more, and a
secession took place to the Dakunugiri Vihāra, where a
new sect, the Sāgaliya, was formed after 794 years had
elapsed since Buddha's death. The heresy was put down
by the king. His son, Jēttha Tissa, signalized his accession and acquired the surname of ' the Cruel ' by impaling
round his father's funeral pyre sixty treasonable ministers.
He built six tanks as well as Mulgirigala Vihāra in Hambantota District, and restored Mutiyangana Vihāra at
Badulla, of which the construction is attributed to Dēvānampiya Tissa. Mahāsēna (Mahasen, fourth century
A.D.), the next son, persecuted the Mahā Vihāra and
favoured the Dharmaruchi fraternity at Abhayagiri.
Later he was reconciled with the orthodox brotherhood,
but offended them by building within their precincts the
Jētavanārāma, now mis-called the Abhayagiri Dāgaba,
for the Sāgaliya sect. He constructed seventeen reservoirs, including Rantisa or Kawdulu-vewa, and the great
Minnēri tank, which he fed by a channel taken off from
the Ambanganga. Padawiya also is attributed to him by
local tradition ; he may have enlarged it. Mahāsēna
has left his mark on the country by his irrigation works,
but has received scant justice from the chronicler, whose
monastery, the Mahā Vihāra, he suppressed. With his
death, after a reign of twenty-seven years, when 844 years
had passed since the Nirvāna, the *Mahāvansa* chronicle
proper ends, a fact perhaps due to the lack of materials
in the monastic archives after the disturbances at Mahā
Vihāra. The termination of the old record is the sole
reason for the division of the kings into the Great and

Lesser Dynasties. Of the so-called ' Great Race ' more than a third ended their days by violence.

The reign of Mahāsēna's son, Siri Mēghavanna (Kit Siri Mevan), is chiefly famous for the arrival of the Tooth Relic in his ninth year, when it was brought from Kalinga to prevent its falling into the hands of a hostile king. According to Chinese authority Siri Mēghavanna was a contemporary of the Indian monarch Samudragupta (c. A.D. 340), to whom he sent presents.

Buddhadāsa (Bujas, fourth century A.D.), of the same dynasty, provided dispensaries throughout the kingdom, and ordained that there should be physicians for every ten villages, the first mention of this ancient grouping (gandahaya) which still survives in name in certain districts. The king also composed in Sanskrit a work on medicine, the Sārartha-sangraha. Strange but impossible stories of operations are recorded of him. His son Upatissa constructed Tōpāvewa.

In the reign of his second son, Mahānāma (fifth century A.D.), the famous commentator Buddhaghōsa came to Ceylon, rewrote the Sinhalese commentaries on the Buddhist scriptures in the Pāli language, and composed the philosophical work Visuddhimagga. In his restatement of religious thought his influence on later Buddhists has been profound. In A.D. 428 a letter from this king was received by the Chinese court : this synchronism postulates an earlier date for the reign than that usually assigned to it.

With Mahānāma the Lambakanna dynasty became extinct. A Pāndyan invasion established foreign rule at Anurādhapura, which is said to have lasted twenty-seven years, but may well have lasted longer. The principal Sinhalese fled to Ruhuna ; here they ultimately found a leader in Dhātusena (Dāsenkeli, late fifth century, A.D.), of the royal Moriyan race, who expelled the Tamils and reunited Ceylon in one sovereignty. His chief work was the construction of the great tank Kalāvewa. His uncle, the priest Mahānāma, was the author of the *Mahāvansa*. He had two sons, Moggallāna and, by a wife of inferior rank, Kassapa. Kassapa (Kāsyapa, or Kasub, sixth century A.D.) rebelled, and seized his father in the hope of securing his treasure. Disappointed in this he buried him alive, and failing to assassinate his brother Moggallāna, who escaped to India, fled to the hill of Sīgiriya. This rises abruptly from the surrounding country and forms an almost impregnable fortress. Kassapa built his palace on the top, an inclined way winding round the rock up to a platform ; here a great lion was constructed, the ascent to the summit passing between its paws. Hence the name Sīgiriya (Sinha-giri, ' lion hill '). The king reigned from his fortress until his eighteenth year, when he was defeated by his brother, and committed suicide. His approximate date is fixed by the receipt at the Chinese court of a letter from him in A.D. 527.

Moggallāna ruled for eighteen years and was succeeded by his son Kumāra Dhātusena, who according to the local tradition was the contemporary and friend of Kālidāsa and threw himself upon the poet's funeral pyre. If Kālidāsa be the Indian bard the synchronism is impossible, as he flourished not later than the middle of the fifth century.

It is convenient in this place to consider Ceylon as it was in the first five centuries of the present era. The innumerable irrigation works at once strike the imagination. The reader, however, must beware of reckoning as new works those merely restored ; the chronicle often makes no difference between the two. The practical certainty that all were not in working order throughout

our period must also be considered.   Nevertheless, those
actually in use at one and the same time must have been
very numerous ; the majority indeed were small, and many
may have been abandoned as the soil was exhausted, new
reservoirs being constructed in their place.   There is no
reason to suppose that the total population of Ceylon was
larger than it is now.   Vast tracts of the country must

FIG. 7.—Sĭgiriya Fresco.

have been in forest, and the more thickly inhabited
centres were in the north, south and south-east of the
Island.   Tamil literature tells us that rice was exported
in early times, but against this has to be set the occurrence
of serious famines, several of which are mentioned in the
chronicles.   Cities in our sense of the word were few, if
indeed Anurādhapura was not the only one ; the capital
was of vast extent, but contained many parks, open spaces
and monastic establishments.   It possessed a quarter

assigned to foreign merchants, in whose hands was most of the trade. About A.D. 500 we read of a Persian Christian colony ; a Nestorian cross undoubtedly belonging to this community is to be seen in the Anurādhapura museum. Traders from Egypt, subjects of the Roman Empire, visited the country, and small Roman copper coins of the fourth century at one time formed the bulk of the currency ; they are found in quantities not only at almost every small port but even at Sīgiriya itself. The chief port of the Island was in the north-west at Mahātittha or Mantota ; about A.D. 500 it was in the hands of an independent prince, just as Colombo was in the fourteenth century.

The earliest alphabet is a local variety of the ' Brahma lipi,' which appears in the inscriptions of Asōka and has its origin in a Semitic script. The most ancient records in Ceylon are met with over caves, and usually consist of a short dedication to the community of monks. In a few the legend still reads from right to left, as in Semitic. For centuries the alphabet developed gradually and on conservative lines. But after the Sīgiriya period the writing becomes so degenerate that it is difficult to distinguish the various letters. The trend towards the modern script began about the eighth or ninth century.

AUTHORITIES FOR CHAPTER II

For general history, see *Dpv.* and *Mhv.*

Ēlāra. For the story of the Chōla king Manu see Hultzsch, ' Contributions to Singhalese Chronology,' *J.R.A.S.*, 1913, p. 530.

Duttha Gāmani. The theory that Vijitapura was in the neighbourhood of Polonnaruwa is elaborated by Parker, *Ancient Ceylon*, pp. 237, 238 ; cf. also *C.A.* x. p. 52.

The construction of Padawiya is attributed to Saddhā Tissa

FIG. 8.—View of Sigiriya across the tank from the South-east.

by the *Puj.* p. 680.   For the Dambulla inscription see *E.Z.* i.
pp. 141, 142 ; but the *Puj.* ascribes Dambulla to Vatta Gāmani.
Vatta Gāmani.   The Tamil invaders are supposed to be
Pāndyan because of the names ending in -māra, the usual
Pāndyan title Māran.   The identification of Abhayagiri with
the dāgaba now known as Jētavanārāma was made by Mr.
Neville (*Ceylon Sessional Papers*, 1914, p. 486, note).
Ila Nāga.   For the inscription identifying the Great Dāgaba
at Tissamahārāma see *A.I.C.* 4 and *C.A.* v. 139.
Vasabha.   The size of Anurādhapura is given in *Puj.* p. 682 ;
it clearly does not refer to the ' Inner City,' which was quite
small.   Tissavaddhamānaka (*Mhv.* xxxv. 84 ; xxxvii. 48) is
identified by the *Puj.* p. 683, with Rantisa tank, and this with the
modern Kawdulu-vewa by the Medirigiriya inscription (*E.Z.* ii.
No. 6) ;   Medirigiriya is not far from Kawdulu-vewa.   The
Elahera (Ālisāra, *Mhv.* xxxv. 84) channel runs through Minnēri
and Kawdulu-vewa into Kantalai.   The Mayetti of *Mhv.* xliv.
90, 101, 102, and li. 131 seems to be identical with the Mayanti,
Chayanti, or Vassanti of Vasabha's reign (*Mhv.* xxxv. 94) ;
it is either Nāchchaduwa tank or the breached reservoir
Ēruvewa.

Gaja Bāhu.   See *Puj.* and its derivative the *Raj.*   For the
king's connection with Pattini worship see *Ancient India*,
S. Krishnaswami Aiyangar, 1911, p. 363.   *J.R.A.S., C.B.* xiii.
No. 44, p. 81, and No. 45, p. 144, should be consulted.

Samudragupta's expedition to the south took place about
A.D. 350 according to Vincent Smith ; but G. Jouveau-
Dubreuil, *Ancient History of the Deccan*, 1920, prefers 340 or
even 335.   For the synchronism of this king with *Siri Mēgha-*
vanna and the Chinese dates for *Mahānāma* and *Kassapa* see
J.R.A.S., C.B. xxiv. No. 68.   If the date given to these two
kings is correct a longer period of Pāndyan rule must be
supposed.   But see ' The Date of Buddhadasa of Ceylon from
a Chinese Source,' E. R. Ayrton, *J.R.A.S.* 1911, p. 1142.   The
attribution of Tōpāvewa to *Upatissa* is made by *Puj.*   For
Kālidāsa's death see *Imperial Gazetteer of India*, Introduction,

p. 333.   The presence of a Persian colony is attested by Cosmas Indicopleustes, *Topographia Christiana*, as also the independence of the principal port.   For a foreign quarter in Anurādhapura see *Ceylon Notes and Queries*, 1913, pt. i. p. viii., and 1914, pt. iv. p. lxii. ; the cross referred to in the text was found in the Inner City.

CHAPTER III

THE MEDIAEVAL KINGDOM TO THE CHOLA CONQUEST IN THE ELEVENTH CENTURY

THE history of the sixth, seventh, and eighth centuries is dull in the extreme ; murder, revolution and civil war are the chief matters of interest.   Yet the later chronicles mention twelve poets as flourishing in the reign of Aggabōdhi I. (A.D. sixth-seventh century).   This king suppressed the Vaitulya heresy, which had been adopted again, nearly forty years before, by the Jētavanārāma monks, and built the great Kurunduvewa, apparently Giants' Tank or Ākattimurippu, besides restoring Mahāsēna's channel to Minnēri, doubtless that known as the Elahera channel.   His nephew, Aggabōdhi II., constructed fourteen tanks, including Kantalai and Giritalē. In his time the king of Kalinga, horrified by war, fled to Ceylon and became a monk : he seems to have been driven from his country by the Chalukya king Pulakēsin II. (A.D. 609-c. 655) possibly about A.D. 609.

King Mānavamma (second half, seventh century) is of importance, partly because from him ' who was skilled in the ways of justice, and born of a pure race, the fountain of all dynasties, and of the lineage of Prince Aggabōdhi and his sons and grandsons, there sprang full sixteen rulers in Lankā,' and partly because of a synchronism

with Indian history.   He was the son of Kassapa II., and
on the overthrow of his family by Dāthōpatissa II. was
obliged shortly after his marriage to fly to India, where
he took service with the Pallava king, Narasinhavarman I.
(A.D. 630-668), and was present at the battle in which this
monarch defeated ' King Vallabha,' the Pulakēsin II.

FIG. 9.—Arankelē Cave Temple.

already mentioned.   This event took place in A.D. 642.
Mānavamma now was helped by the Pallava king to
recover the kingdom of Ceylon from Dāthōpatissa, but
though he succeeded in taking Anurādhapura was compelled to return to India, where he remained during the
three following reigns.   Narasinhavarman claims that he
conquered Lankā ; his grandfather Sinhavishnu also is
said to have defeated among others the Sinhalese king
(roughly A.D. 575-600).
    It is stated that in the year 790 during the reign of

Dappula II. there arrived, wafted across the sea to Dondra, the red sandal-wood image of Vishnu, which afterwards was taken to Alutnuwara in Kēgalla District, and still later to the Maha Dēwālē in Kandy. According to another tradition Dondra temple was built by Aggabōdhi IV. (middle of seventh century). Polonnaruwa is mentioned first as a royal residence in this reign.

The next king of importance is Sēna I., who according to a later chronicle came to the throne in A.B. 1362 or A.D. 819/20, a date apparently obtained by reckoning backwards from Parākrama Bāhu the Great the reigns as given in the *Pujāvaliya*.

In this king's time the Pāndyans invaded Ceylon in force, the Tamils resident in the country joined them, and Ānurādhapura itself was

FIG. 10.—Mediaeval Gold Coin.

sacked. The later chronicles state that the Tooth and Bowl Relics were carried off; but there appears to be no authority for this. Sēna returned to Ānurādhapura, peace having been made with the Pāndyans, but he afterwards left it for Polonnaruwa where he died, having reigned twenty years. Polonnaruwa from this time forward became the capital. The late king's nephew, Sēna II. (ninth century), succeeded him, and in his ninth year his general invaded the Pāndyan country, took and sacked Madura, and set on the throne a pretender, the Tamil monarch having died of wounds received in battle. Sēna suppressed various heretical sects, which had appeared in Ceylon in his predecessor's time, and placed guards round the coast to prevent the entry of their adherents ; he died in his thirty-fifth year, leaving the throne to his brother Udaya I. who in his turn was succeeded by Kassapa IV.

Kassapa V. (ninth-tenth century), ' born of the twice-crowned queen ' Sangha, was the son of Sēna II., and was made sub-king at his birth. He was a man of learning, and wrote a Sinhalese paraphrase of the *Dhammapada*, which still survives. In his reign the Pāndyan king Rājasinha unwisely made war on the Chōlas, and being routed asked for Kassapa's help. The Sinhalese king thereupon sent an army, which returned to Ceylon unsuccessful. He died according to the *Mahāvansa* in his tenth year. His successor, Dappula IV. only ruled for a few months, and Dappula V. (early tenth century) had hardly come to the throne when the Pāndyan king arrived in Ceylon, flying from the Chōlas. The Sinhalese monarch was preparing to give him help when a sudden strife arose among the princes of the Island, and the Pandyan had to retire to Malabar disappointed, leaving, however, his crown and royal ornaments with the king of Ceylon. The war between the Pāndyans and Chōlas seems to have taken place at the end of the reign of Kassapa V. and at the beginning of that of Dappula V. ; the invasion of Rājasinha and the king of Ceylon actually is mentioned in a record of the Chōla king Parāntaka I. (A.D. 907-953) dated in his twelfth year, or A.D. 918/9. We see here the rise of the great Chōla Empire, which first overshadowed and finally engulfed the Island kingdom.

After Udaya II. and Sēna III. the Sinhalese throne was occupied by Udaya III., who was ' a drunkard and a sluggard.' Parāntaka took advantage of this, and sent an embassy for the Pāndyan regalia left in Ceylon in the time of Dappula V. His demand being refused, he invaded the Island, Udaya flying with the disputed regalia towards Ruhuna, which the Chōla army did not succeed in entering. The enemy then ' returned to their own country, leaving the Island in great fear,' and Udaya took

reprisals by destroying ' the borders of the dominion of
the king of Chōla.' Parāntaka's power was broken by
the Rāshtrakūta king Krishna III. about A.D. 942/3,
and it seems likely that this was the cause of the Chōla
retreat and the counter-invasion of the Sinhalese. Udaya

FIG. 11.—Western Monastery I. (after restoration),
Anurādhapura.

died in his eighth year, while rebuilding a palace burnt
by the Chōlas.

Udaya's second successor was his nephew Mahinda IV.
(middle of tenth century). He departed from former
custom by marrying a princess of the ruling family of
Kalinga, which in the twelfth century gave a dynasty to
the Island. Before his ninth year Ceylon was attacked
by King Vallabha, apparently the Chōla king Parāntaka
II., whose general was slain in Ceylon about A.D. 960.
The enemy army landed at Ūrātota (Kayts). This was the

last success of the Sinhalese for many a long year, as
Mahinda's son Sēna V. foolishly murdered his general's
brother, and the enraged officer took his revenge by
assembling together the Tamils settled in Ceylon and
making over the country to them. This took place in the
second year of the reign. The Tamils so oppressed the
people that Sēna made his peace with the general and
returned to Polonnaruwa. Here, however, becoming
addicted to strong drink, and ' like unto a mad tiger,' he
died while still young, in the tenth year of his reign, and
was succeeded by his brother Mahinda V. or Udaya
(tenth-eleventh century).

The new king reigned at Anuradhapura but governed
with difficulty, as the city was full of foreigners introduced
by his late brother's general. In his twelfth year the
revenue was withheld and the king was unable to pay his
Malabar mercenaries, who mutinied. Mahinda thereupon
fled to Ruhuna, leaving the country in the hands of the
Malabars, Sinhalese, and Canarese. The opportunity was
too good to be lost, and at some date between A.D. 1001/2
and 1004/5 the great Chōla emperor Rājarāja I. (A.D.
985-1012) conquered all the country, save the remoter
parts which were still held by the Sinhalese. The conquest
was completed about A.D. 1017 by the capture of Mahinda
V. himself with his crown jewels and the Pāndyan regalia
left by Rājasinha. Ceylon became a province of the
Chōla empire and Polonnaruwa was renamed Jananātha-
pura. It was at this period that many of the Hindu
shrines in the city were erected. Mahinda V. died in
captivity in India.

The ninth and tenth centuries are signalized by a pro-
fusion of inscriptions, which in the later part of the period
show some elegance of composition. As a whole, however,
they give little historical information, and compare

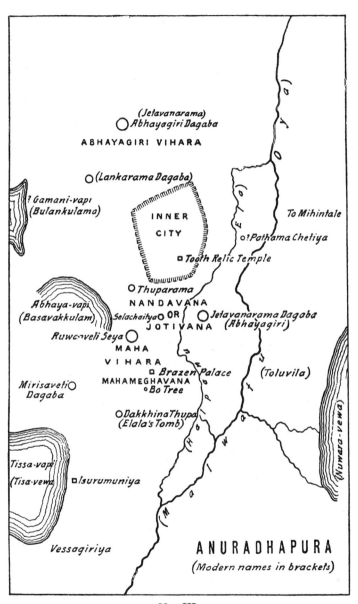

MAP III.

unfavourably in this respect with those of South India. The alphabet develops rapidly in the direction of the modern character in the ninth century and in the early years of the tenth. Fines were paid in gold bullion as on the mainland and money was scarce, but the period was marked by the issue of a gold coinage, which, however, speedily degenerated in the fineness of the metal used. Medical establishments existed in the villages. On the whole the general impression left on the mind is one of prosperity, perhaps more solid than that of the superficially more brilliant reign of Parākrama Bāhu I. As in Southern India the sovereigns bore alternately two throne names, to wit, Siri Sangabo and Abhā Salamevan (Abhaya Silāmēgha-varna), a custom which can be traced in Ceylon as far back as the seventh century.

THE ADMINISTRATION.

The records of the period are mainly concerned with temples and we know little of the constitution of the realm. A council undoubtedly existed just as one did in the last days of the Kandyan kingdom, but we can only guess at its functions. Doubtless custom was all-powerful. The succession to the throne normally seems not to have been from father to son, but from one brother to another, and then to the son of the eldest brother and his brothers. Next to the king came the sub-king (Yuvaraja, ' young king,' Māpā or Mahayā), who usually held the ' Southern Country ' as his appanage. Ruhuna was governed by an Ēpā, a title held by more than one of the royal family. The ' Southern Country ' and Ruhuna appear to have been to a great degree autonomous. We also hear of the Senevirad or Commander-in-chief, a member of the royal family, and of Dandanāyakas or generals : the army contained foreign mercenaries, usually Tamils. Anurādhapura was in charge of an officer, the Nuwara-laddā. The village communities doubtless enjoyed very great independence, as was the case in South India. Royal control was exercised by officials, who went on circuit annually, somewhat in the manner of the English assizes, to administer justice and collect the king's dues, and this was still done as late as the early seventeenth century.

A feature of the time was the large extent of temple property. The temple administration was controlled by

FIG. 12.—Moonstone, ' Queen's Pavilion,' Anurādhapura.

the priests through the means of lay wardens and a host of officials. The villages enjoyed considerable immunities ; by these no royal officer could impress coolies, carts and oxen, or cut down trees, or remove criminals who had taken sanctuary. Varying provisions applied to murderers ; in some cases they were driven out and arrested outside the village limits, in others they were to be tried and punished with exile. In one instance provision was made that public officers might enter and demand their surrender only, and that on the expiry of every two years the royal officials on circuit might require the persons of the perpetrators of ' the five great crimes,' but not others. Offenders who had committed lesser offences seem to have had safe sanctuary. The privileges above mentioned touching forced service and felling of fruit trees, in one instance specifically given as palmyrahs and coconut-trees, form an illuminating commentary on the conditions existing outside the temple lands.

On the other hand, strict regulations existed for the control of crime in the temple villages. The headmen and householders had to give security. In the case of murder they were bound to enquire, record evidence, and have the murderer killed; in one of housebreaking they had to restore the goods to the owner and have the thieves hanged. If the criminals were not detected, the village on failure to have them punished within forty-five days was liable to a fine of 125 kalandas of gold, about 1½ lb. troy, a large sum for those days. In cases of violent assault not involving loss of life the fine or ' life-price ' was 50 kalandas, which the village also had to pay on failure to punish the crime. The penalty for killing oxen was death ; cattle thieves were branded under the arm-pits. Cattle could only be brought into the village after identification and the taking of security, while the effacer of brandmarks was compelled to stand upon red-hot sandals. Identification and security were also insisted on in the case of villagers coming from outside. Failure of the village in these matters was dealt with by the royal officers on their annual circuit.

We may now consider the system of land tenure pre-valent during the ninth and tenth centuries. The technical terms in the inscriptions would be scarcely intelligible but for the analogies offered by South India, and in particular by Malabar ; the whole subject requires further study. In the Indian land system ' traditionally there were two parties, and only two, to be taken into account ; these parties were the ruler and the subject, and if a subject occupied land, he was required to pay a share of its gross produce to the ruler in return for the protection he was entitled to receive ' ; [1] in addition the village commonly supplied an amount of unpaid labour (Ūliyam) for the service of the king or lord. Further, there were numerous grants of the revenue due from particular villages or plots of land in favour of temples, charitable institutions, or individuals. Such grants often were expressed in terms implying perpetuity, but ' in practice they were always resumable at the pleasure of the ruler of the day ; and under native rule there was a continual process of resuming old grants, and granting new ones.' [2]

The tenth century system seems to have been in no way different from that of the mainland. The body of the tenants (kudīn) in a temple village held land on ' instrument ' (kere) tenure, and paid a proportion of the crop to the lord. The ' instrument ' perhaps was analogous to the running statement of account (patta) in Mysore. Presumably the kudīn were tenants-at-will, as was the case in India in theory until recent days, but the Mihintalē Tablets forbid the removal of ' cultivators ' who held their fields by ' Cultivator succession.' Thus heritable holdings among tenants had already begun. As might be expected the policy of non-interference with succession is found first in the case of the peasant, who was too insignificant for the lord's notice. The process was a gradual one, and even at the end of the Dutch period the more important lands held by service tenure were

[1] *India at the Death of Akbar*, W. H. Moreland, 1920, p. 96.

[2] *System of Land Tenures in various Countries*, Cobden Club, 1870, p. 148.

still not heritable, while the holdings of the village servants
and others had become so, provided, of course, that the
service was performed. In the tenth century the lord's
officials and the village headmen (*kemiyan*) were paid for
their service by ' maintenance ' (*divel*) lands, as were also
the temple slaves and village servants. The ordinary
holding of a mason in such a village was 1½ kiriyas (6 acres)
of paddy land, an enclosure or dwelling garden, and a plot
of high land. Some if not all of the above tenants would
seem to be those styled ' holders of allotments ' (*kebeli-
laduvan*), who not being complete owners were not
entitled to fell jungle.

Above these tenures we find Pātta or Gam-pātta.
Details are lacking, but the holders, if the Gam-laddan of
the inscriptions, clearly held a superior position. From
the analogy of the Malabar kāna-pāttam, we may conclude
that the land so held paid assessment, but that the tenant
was in possession for a number of years, and could obtain
renewal of the lease.

The superior tenures were Pamunu (' possession ') and
Ukas ('mortgage'). Pamunu were granted by the king,
or, in his principality by the sub-king, under seal, and
included all grants to temples and charitable institutions
as well as those to important chiefs ; in the case of the
last named a small quit rent was often, if not always,
imposed in the form of a payment of oil to the Tooth
Relic or to some temple. Pamunu holders had full rights
over the jungle on their lands. Judging from Indian
practice it would depend on the wording of the grant
whether the land conveyed was alienable or heritable or
both. The Ukas has to be compared with the Malabar
Otti or usufructuary mortgage. Outright sale is considered disgraceful ; hence a mortgage, under which the
payer of the money enters into possession of the land,

while the original owner retains an indefinite right of re-entry on payment of the debt. Outside temple villages and those similarly alienated there are still in Travancore lands in which the State is in the position of constructive mortgagor. Though the tenure survived in some Tamil districts it has disappeared from the Sinhalese country. We know practically nothing of the land tenure outside the temple villages, but there can be little doubt that in the main features there was no difference and that the king merely took the place of the priestly overlord.

It is convenient in this place to complete our review of the land tenures of Ceylon. In the twelfth century we find the provincial governors described as being in charge of the ' asampandi,' possibly a Tamil form of the Hindustani jamabandi or ' land assessment.' Nissanka Malla claims to have reduced the excessive demands of his predecessors and fixed the revenue (*aya*) at $1\frac{3}{4}$ amunams on the amunam sowing extent for the best paddy land, at $1\frac{1}{2}$ for that of medium quality, and at $1\frac{1}{4}$ for the poorest ; the additional cash payments were fixed at six, four, and three ' aka ' coins respectively. The Hindu law books regard the demand of $\frac{1}{6}$ or $\frac{1}{12}$ as reasonable, a tax of $\frac{1}{4}$ being sanctioned only in emergencies. Taking the average yield of the best paddy land other than under the great tanks as fifteen-fold, we find that Nissanka's revenue therefrom amounted to 11 per cent. At the same time he appears to have exempted from taxation chena land, that is, jungle land periodically burnt and cultivated. Of course his regulation did not bind his successors, and we know that chena land paid its quota in the early seventeenth century.

History often recounts the grant of men and women slaves with other movable property to temples. The unpublished documents connected with the dedication of

land to Pepiliyāna Vihāra in the fifteenth century show that
these slaves were largely artisans, blacksmiths, potters,
lime-burners, and the like, and doubtless the slaves
of the tenth century already referred to performed similar
duties. The tenants of the king's villages in the early
seventeenth century are definitely stated to have been
slaves, and their presence in the royal and temple villages,
though long forgotten, accounts for the low esteem in
which the tenants on those properties are still held.

With the Portuguese administration the Sinhalese land
system is seen in all its detail. The village usually consisted of the holdings (*wedawasam, divel*), possessed by the
cultivation headmen or mayorals and the village servants,
such as the blacksmiths, potters and the like. These
holdings were indivisible, often heritable in the male line
only, and liable to escheat to the Crown or to the lord in
default of performance of service. The balance of the
village was divided among the rest of the population, who
paid a share (*otu*) of the produce of their fields, varying with
the locality from one to two amunams on each amunam
sown ; the highest yield given in the Tombo is twelve-fold.
These lands were heritable and alienable and seem to
have descended in the male or female line. In addition
in many villages there was the home demesne (*muttettu*)
of the king or lord, cultivated free of cost by certain
tenants. The villages in most cases were given to individuals for life or for a term of lives, when the temporary
lord enjoyed the produce of the home demesne, was
entitled to the services of the people, and received various
payments at their hands as well as the *otu* share. The
holder of the village paid a foro or rent to the Crown,
calculated at twelve per cent. of the revenue. The
holdings both of the temporary lord and of the tenants
other than payers of *otu* were known to the Portuguese

by the name of ' comedia,' or ' maintenance.' Gardens in some cases were taxed at the rate of one silver fanam on every ten coconut trees, an impost which was supposed to equal a tenth of the produce ; it may, perhaps, be presumed that these gardens formed part of the holdings of the *otu*-paying population, while those which paid nothing belonged to the service holdings proper. The chenas also paid their quota. As in India all land paid in kind or in service.

In Jaffna, where the older system survived, the people paid a share of the produce, rendered labour, and paid a poll tax. Certain lands were given by the king for life, and in these and others which had escheated a marāla or death duty became inherent, and was exacted at every succession for a re-grant to the heir. A marāla, amounting usually to one-third of the deceased's movables, or, if no male heir had been left, to the whole, was levied in the Sinhalese country on all estates. This custom was not peculiar to Ceylon, and in India told with much severity on the great men, all of whose movables usually were seized by the king at death. The principle underlying this impost was the royal claim to the soil, a claim also seen in the Tamil and Sinhalese countries in the recovery of the ' soil-burning ' fee (*bim pulutu*) before the cremation of a dead body was allowed. In its origin it seems to have been analogous to the renewal fees on pāttam leases in Malabar. In Ceylon, however, it practically became a tax on succession. In the Kandyan country it was not levied on women, and was abolished about the middle of the eighteenth century, though the last king revived it in its most severe form at least on the death of one chief.

The two features of the Sinhalese system, as developed by the seventeenth century, were firstly the complete merger of the lands paying a share of the crop in the service tenure system, and secondly, the gradual conversion of the great majority of holdings into heritable (*paraveni*) tenure, subject to performance of services and payment of succession duty and in many cases to considerable limitations in the disposition of the property.

FIG. 13.—Wata-dā-gē, Medirigiriya.

It was the *otu* payers, not being liable to service involving technical knowledge peculiar to one class, who benefited most.

The colonization of the North and East of the Island by Hindu Tamils seems to have been due quite as much to peaceful penetration as to war. In many places it is sufficiently recent to have preserved the Sinhalese village names in a form which cannot be older than the Middle Ages. Presumably during the period under review as in later times trade was in their hands and in those of the local Muhammadans, now known by the Portuguese designation of Moor, who may be the Mēlātsi (Mēlēchchha) of the tenth century inscriptions. Muslims are first heard of in Ceylon in the late seventh century, and gold coins of most of the dynasties of Egypt and Hither Asia from that time, but in particular of the twelfth and thirteenth centuries, are found in the west of the Island. It was during these two centuries that the Muhammadans attained the height of their commercial prosperity and political influence in Southern India. The presence of Chinese traders is attested by coins dating from the tenth to the thirteenth century.

In concluding this chapter we may note the periodical recrudescence of Mahāyānist forms of Buddhism, which in particular infected the Abhayagiri community. It is perhaps to the influence of these doctrines that the worship of the Hindu gods in the popular Buddhism of the present day is due.

AUTHORITIES FOR CHAPTER III

For general history see *Mhv.* and *Puj.*

Aggabōdhi I. The list of the poets appears in *Puj.* and derivative works. Kurundu-vewa is identified tentatively with Giants' Tank or Ākattimurippu as the lower course of the Malwatu Oya was known as Kurundu Oya (Knox, *Relation of Ceylon,* part iv. chap. x.), and the Kurundu country seems to have been in this neighbourhood ; see *C.A.* x. p. 94.

Aggabōdhi II. For Pulakēsin II. and his relations with Kalinga see Jouveau-Dubreuil, *op. cit.* p. 93, who places the conquest in 609.

Mānavamma. For his dealings with Narasinhavarman I. see Hultzsch, *op. cit.* pp. 527 ff. The identification of the Pallava king with Narasinhavarman II. (630-668) is almost certainly wrong, as it would make the period between Māna-

vamma and Sēna I. far too short. For the claim of Sinhavishnu see *S.I.I.* ii. 356.

The date of the foundation of Dondra by *Dappula II.* is
given in a Sanskrit sloka, which works out correctly after an
obvious emendation.

No certain remains of a palace can be traced at Anurādhapura except those of a mediaeval building, and the occupation of Polonnaruwa as a royal seat may have been due to the
overwhelming predominance of the priesthood and the consequent desire for freedom on the part of the king. This
supposition would account for Ptolemy's description of Anurogrammon as ' the royal city ' and of Maagrammon as ' the
metropolis.' The name Maagrammon of course corresponds
with the modern Mahanuwara, ' the capital.' I have already
thrown out the suggestion that Maagrammon may have been
in the neighbourhood of the later Polonnaruwa. But Maagrammon and Polonnaruwa may have stood in the same
relation to Anurādhapura as Nillambē, Hanguranketa and
Kundasālē to Kandy.

The date of the accession of *Sēna I.* is given in *N.S.* For
the ninth year of Sēna II. see inscriptions at Ellēvewa, *A.I.C.*
116 ; Bilibēwa, *E.Z.* ii. No. 8 ; Etāvīragollēwa, *ib.* No. 9.

Varagunavarman, son of Srī Vallabha, apparently the
Pāndyan king who invaded Ceylon under Sēna I., came to the
throne between March and November A.D. 862. This does
not necessarily mark Sēna II.'s ninth year, as the prince set on
the throne of Madura by his general may not have been a son
of the deceased king. For the pedigree and date mentioned
see Sinnamanūr Plates (*A.R.E.* 1907, para. 6 ff.), Velvikudi
grant (*ib.* 1908, para. 15 ff.), and *Epigraphia Indica*, xi. No. 24,
p. 253.

Kassapa V. and Dappula V. For Rājasinha and Parāntaka
see *A.R.E.* 1907, pp. 72, 73, and Udayendiram Plates, *S.I.I.*
ii. 387. For Krishna III. see *Ep. Ind.* iv. No. 40, and
' Critical Notes on the Epigraphia Zeylanica,' *C.A.* iv. pt. i.
p. 35.

Mahinda IV. For the ninth year see Vessagiriya inscription, *E.Z.*, i. No. 2. ' Vallabha ' was a Chōla title, and I am now inclined to the identification made in the text rather than to that with Krishna III. put forward in *C.A.* iv. pt. i. p. 35. For the general of Parāntaka II. see *A.R.E.* 1914, p. 90. *Sēna V.* The *Puj.* dates the commencement of Tamil rule from the sixth of the waxing moon of Durutu of this king's second year.

Mahinda V. He may be the Udaya mentioned in *Mhv.* liv. 58. The Sorabora-vewa pillar inscription, now in Badulla, of the reign of Siri Sang Bo Udā may be of this period from the epigraphic point of view. For the Chōla conquest see *S.I.I.* iii. 6 and 52 ; an inscription of the twenty-seventh year of Rājarāja I. is at Padawiya. For Chōla records in Ceylon see *A.S.* 1907, 1909, and for the Chōla name of Polonnaruwa, *ib.* 1906, p. 27 ; 1909, p. 27.

The order of succession to the throne is deduced from *Mhv.* The Yuvaraja normally seems to have been the next brother of the reigning king, or in default the eldest prince of the next generation. For the Nuwara-laddā see the Basavakkulam inscription of the nineteenth year of Sēna II., now in Colombo Museum. For the assizes and temple immunities, *E.Z.* i. pp. 244-53 *et passim,* may be consulted ; similar immunities appear in a grant to a layman subject to payment of a quitrent to a temple (*E.Z.* ii. No. 4). The fruit trees are mentioned in the Kapuru Vedu Oya inscription, published in *J.R.A.S., C.B.,* xxvi. No. 71, pt. i. p. 53. The collapse of the old village community perhaps was gradual and the individualistic tendency encouraged by the movement of the population from the dry zone, where the village still is an agglomeration of houses close to the tank bund, to the wetter country, in which each man sat ' under his own fig tree.' But even in the early nineteenth century communal responsibility survived in certain cases. Thus the village was fined when a man committed suicide in an inhabited area, but not when he did so in the jungle.

Land Tenure. The *Cambridge History of India* (p. 475)

with reference to the Maurya Empire says, ' Apart from the royal domains . . . the ultimate property in the land appertained, in the sense which has since prevailed, to the King : that is to say, the King was entitled to his revenues therefrom, and in default could replace the cultivator in his holding. This does not preclude alienation or subdivision by the occupier, the royal title persisting through each change.'

Examples of resumptions of grants in Ceylon are Gilīmalē, once dedicated by Vijaya Bāhu I., for the supply of food to pilgrims to Adam's Peak, and Kendangamuwa, given by Parākrama Bāhu VI. to Aramanapola Vihāra. Both under the Kandyan Government were royal villages.

Pāttam in Malayalam and modern Tamil is ' rent ' ; in older Tamil it is ' assessment tax.' It exactly equals the Sinhalese ' badda,' which has both meanings, and illustrates the difficulty of ' disentangling the conception of private right from political allegiance which has made so much progress during the last century ' (Moreland, op. cit., p. 96). For the holding of a mason see E.Z. i. No. 1. For grants to laymen see E.Z. ii. No. 4, and the Doratiyāwa tudupata (twelfth century) in J.R.A.S., C.B. xxix. No. 77. For the technical terms see E.Z. i. Nos. 7 and 8 ; for ' asampandi,' J.R.A.S., C.B. ib., and for Nissanka Malla's taxation, E.Z. i. No. 9. The words uttē, menda, and pessē, which I have rendered by ' best,' ' medium,' and ' poorest,' are found in the Pepiliyāna documents in the expressions uttē taramin, meddē taramin, and pessē taramin ; the use of maddama tarama in Wellassa shows that we must understand these words with reference to irrigation facilities. Nissanka's exemption of chena lands from taxation is not devoid of difficulty. The language used in the series of documents in which the concession is recorded seems to imply that it was limited to cases where jungle was felled for the purpose of forming rice fields. Further investigation is desirable. For the slaves in the royal villages see the petition from the Sinhalese in 1636 given at length in De Q. p. 834. For polaya, the garden tax, see the Portuguese Tombo,

and Valentyn, *Oud en Nieuw Oost Indien*, v. 268. For the
Marāla see *De Q.* pp. 41, 42, 76, 80, 842 ; *Documentos remettidos
da India*, ii. pp. 82, 136 ; Valentyn, pp. 10, 269, 270 ; Knox,
Interior of Ceylon, pt. ii. chap. iv. v. and pt. iii., chap. vii. ; for
Jaffna, the Foral. For the comedias in general see *De Q.*
p. 80. The Portuguese *Tombo* marks holdings as paraveni
(hereditary) but rarely, but the great majority were popularly
claimed to be of this tenure, judging from the use of the word
in Ribeiro, *Fatalidade Historica*, and in the petition of 1636 ;
see also *Instructions from the Governor General*, Government
Press, 1908, pp. 40, 61. In the Portuguese *Tombo* paraveni
is distinguished from purchased land. The late Kandyan
system as given by D'Oyly is reproduced in the *Report on the
Kēgalla District, Sessional Papers*, xix. 1892, pp. 107 ff. The
' head-money ' (*is-ran*) directed by the Daladā Sirita to be
paid to the Tooth Relic may represent the Jaffna poll tax.

For the Mahāyānist teachings see *N.S.* Also A. M. Hocart,
' The Thuparama Temple at Anuradhapura,' Notes and Queries,
in *J.R.A.S., C.B.* xxviii. No. 73, p. 57. The so-called
Kushtarāja statue at Weligama is supposed to represent
Avalōkitēsvara.

CHAPTER IV

THE POLONNARUWA KINGS, 1070-1215

THE years following the deportation of Mahinda V. were
filled with abortive risings by the Sinhalese alternating with
repression by the Chōlas. At first the captive king's son
Kassapa or Vikrama Bāhu led the national resistance.
On his death anarchy supervened, Sinhalese adventurers
and dispossessed Indian princes from the Pāndyan
country, and even one Jagatipāla from Kanauj asserting
authority over portions of the Island. Finally the hopes

of the Sinhalese centred in the person of the young prince
Kitti, who was born about A.D. 1039. When fifteen years
of age he defeated the last pretender, Lōkissara, and on
attaining his majority at sixteen assumed the rank of
sub-king with the name of Vijaya Bāhu. His attention
now was given entirely to the liberation of his country.

FIG. 14.—Siva Dēwālē, No. 2, Polonnaruwa.

A first attempt to secure Polonnaruwa was made in or
about A.D. 1066 but ended in failure, and Vijaya Bāhu
was compelled to fortify himself at Vātagiri (Wākirigala
in Kēgalla District). Rebellion as usual hampered the
young prince, but at last an opportunity presented itself
in the civil war, which raged in the Chōla empire and
ended with the accession of Kulōttunga Chōla I. in A.D.
1069/70. Vijaya Bāhu was then at Mahānāgakula on the
lower Walawē Ganga, and dispatched two armies, one by

' the highway by the sea,' through the Eastern Province, and one to the west of the mountain system, while he himself advanced by Mahiyangana. Polonnaruwa fell, and Anurādhapura was entered in the prince's fifteenth year, about A.D. 1070. His coronation as monarch of Lankā was delayed by rebellion, and only took place in his eighteenth year, or A.D. 1072/3. Polonnaruwa now lost its Chōla title and was styled Vijayarājapura. Vijaya Bāhu married Līlāvatī, daughter of Jagatipāla of Kanauj, whose queen had escaped from captivity in the Chōla country, and also Tilōkasundarī of the Kalinga royal race, while his sister Mittā espoused a Pāndyan prince, who became the grandfather of Parākrama Bāhu the Great. The king restored the Buddhist religion, renewing the priestly succession from Rāmañña (Pegu), and caused a temple for the Tooth Relic to be built at the capital by his general Nuvaragiri.

The mutilation of ambassadors sent by Vijaya Bāhu to the West Chalukya king Vikramāditya VI. by the Chōlas led to a declaration of war. Preparations were being made about A.D. 1084/5, when the Vēlakkāra mercenaries, unwilling to fight their Tamil kinsmen, mutinied, and burnt the royal palace. The king fled to Wākirigala, but returning crushed the insurrection, the ringleaders being burnt at the funeral pyre of the royal generals whom they murdered. The Vēlakkāra force learnt the lesson, and at the end of the reign set up the fine Tamil stone inscription still extant at Polonnaruwa, in which is recorded their agreement to protect the Tooth Relic temple.

Almost the last act of this king was the construction of resting-places on the roads to Adam's Peak, and the grant of the village of Gilīmalē in Ratnapura District for the purpose of supplying food to pilgrims. This benefaction is recorded in a large rock inscription at

Ambagamuwa, not far from Nāwalapitiya, dated in the thirty-eighth year from his coronation as sole king. Vijaya Bāhu reigned fifty-five years, and died at the age of seventy-two, about A.D. 1111.

His successor was his brother Jaya Bāhu (1108-1145/6), the sub-king, who had been promoted to this office on the death of his elder brother Vīra Bāhu apparently towards the end of the reign. As a Tamil inscription at Polonnaruwa equates the thirty-eighth year of Jaya Bāhu with the fifteenth of Gaja Bāhu, it is probable that this king was Vijaya's half brother. The coronation of Jaya Bāhu was carried out by the Pāndyan faction in the royal family, who took advantage of the absence of Vikrama Bāhu of the Kalinga party as governor of Ruhuna, and the office of sub-king at the same time was conferred on Mānābharana or Vīra Bāhu, one of the three sons of the Pāndyan prince and Vijaya Bāhu's sister Mittā ; by this appointment they ' transgressed the ancient customs,' the office by right belonging to the king's own brother or the late king's son. Jaya Bāhu's kingship seems to have been strictly legal, as Vikrama Bāhu, though he deprived him of power, never assumed the crown himself, and documents were dated in Jaya Bāhu's regnal years even at Polonnaruwa. The Pāndyan party at once proceeded to attack Vikrama Bāhu, but were beaten ; the prince went to the capital, and Jaya Bāhu retired to Ruhuna, where he lived as nominal sovereign and subsequently died in obscurity.

The country was now divided into four parts. The ' King's Country,' with its capital at Polonnaruwa was held by Vikrama Bāhu (1111-1132) ; he seized the lands dedicated to Buddha and oppressed the priests, who removed the Tooth and Bowl Relics to Ruhuna. The ' Southern Country ' was ruled by Mānābharana, while Ruhuna was divided between the other two brothers, Siri

Vallabha having Dolosdahas-rata, roughly the Southern Province, and Kitti Sirimēgha Atadahas-rata or the modern Uva and most of the Eastern Province.

Mānābharana's famous son Parākrama Bāhu was born at Punkhagāma in the ' Southern Country,' and after his father's death retired with his mother to Mahānāgakula in the dominions of his uncle, Siri Vallabha, who now ruled the whole of Ruhuna on his surviving brother succeeding to Mānābharana's principality. On the death of Vikrama Bāhu, after a rule of twenty-one years, and the accession of his son, Gaja Bāhu II. (A.D. 1131-1153), Siri Vallabha and Kitti Sirimēgha attacked the ' King's Country,' but failed in their enterprise. Parākrama Bāhu had now grown up and went to the country of his birth, where he lived at his uncle's court. His ambitious spirit made him restless and discontented with the prospect of ruling a petty principality. Accordingly one night he left the court and went to Batalagoda, where the general in command was killed, and thence through Hiriyāla to Buddhagāma (Menikdena Nuwara in Mātalē District), where he intrigued with Gaja Bāhu's general at Kalāvewa. His uncle, fearing complications with the Court of Polonnaruwa, sent troops to bring him back, but the prince, making a detour through Bōgambara and Ranamurē in the Laggala country of Mātalē East and through Ambana, finally crossed the frontier and so came to Polonnaruwa : here he lived with Gaja Bāhu, and spent his time in spying out the country, and intriguing with his host's subjects. Later he returned to his uncle, and succeeded him on his death.

As ruling prince he did much to improve his dominions by the construction of irrigation works, particularly on the Deduru Oya, and by the organization of the military and civil government. Having consolidated his position,

he attacked Gaja Bāhu, first annexing Dumbara and the
adjoining hill country. In the campaign which followed
most of the fighting took place in the present Mātalē
District. Finally Polonnaruwa was stormed and Gaja
Bāhu himself captured. Mānābharana, who had succeeded
his father Siri Vallabha in Ruhuna, now came to the
rescue, defeated Parākrama Bāhu's army and set Gaja
Bāhu at liberty. But the king had found a worse master
in Mānābharana, and appealed to Parākrama Bāhu for
help. War ensued, and Gaja Bāhu, again at liberty, fled,
while his officers fought with his deliverer. Ultimately
he abdicated in favour of Parākrama Bāhu, and died at
Kantalai after a reign of twenty-two years. His ministers,
however, sent for Mānābharana, while Parākrama hurried
to Polonnaruwa and was crowned. A campaign of varying
fortune ensued, ending in the defeat of Mānābharana, who
fled to his own country and died. Parākrama Bāhu
thereupon was crowned a second time.

Parākrama Bāhu the Great (A.D. 1153-1186) was now
sole monarch of Ceylon, but his rule was not acceptable
to all. In his fourth year (A.D. 1156/7) Sugalā Dēvī,
mother of Mānābharana, raised the standard of revolt in
Ruhuna. The campaign against the rebels was pro-
tracted ; in the early part of it the Tooth and Bowl Relics
were recovered and dispatched to Polonnaruwa. The
rebels gradually were driven to the south of the Island by
the royal army operating in Uva, and their defeat was
ensured by the arrival of other forces from Sabaragamuwa
and the western sea coast. Sugalā Dēvī herself was
captured and the revolt collapsed. Ruhuna for the
moment was quiet, but rose again in the king's eighth
year or A.D. 1160/1.

In his twelfth year (A.D. 1164/5) Parākrama Bāhu went
to war with the king of Rāmañña (Pegu), disputes having

Fig. 15.—Statue of " Parākrama Bāhu," Polonnaruwa.

arisen on the subject of the elephant trade and the treatment of the Sinhalese ambassadors ; the crowning offence was the seizure of a princess sent from Ceylon to Cambodia.

A fleet was collected at the port of Paluvak-tota, perhaps Palvakki on the coast north of Trincomalee ; it set sail in the south-west monsoon and the sailors stormed the city of Kusumiya (Cosmin on the Pegu River). There the army remained for five months, when, the king of Rāmañña having been slain, peace was restored. The grant of land given to the general Kit Nuvaragiri (Kitti Nagaragiri), is recorded in a rock inscription at Devanagala in Kēgalla District.

After this expedition and before A.D. 1167/8 the Pāndyan king Parākrama Pāndya, being besieged by the Chōla king Kulasēkhara, sent for help to Ceylon. The Sinhalese monarch thereupon sent an army under his general Lankāpura, but in the meantime the Pāndyan king had been slain and his capital Madura taken. The Sinhalese army, however, landed on the opposite coast, and carried on the war against the Chōlas in the neighbourhood of Rāmnād, where they built a fortress styled Parākramapura. The result of this stage of the campaign was the defeat of Kulasēkhara and the restoration and crowning of the Pāndyan king's son, Vīra Pāndya, in his ancient capital. The captives taken by the army were sent to Ceylon and employed in repairs to the Ruwanweli Dāgaba, which had been broken down by the Chōlas during their rule in the Island. Whether the Sinhalese ultimately were so successful as made out by the *Mahāvansa* is more than doubtful ; the Chōla records claim that Lankāpura was defeated and his head nailed to the gates of Madura with those of his generals. The war of the Pāndyan secession did not end here : in the thirteenth year of the Chōla king Rājādhirāja II. (A.D. 1175/6) we hear of Sinhalese victories, and by the fourth year of Kulōttunga Chōla III. (1181/2) Vīra Pāndya had been expelled, and the Sinhalese soldiers driven into the sea. But the

FIG. 16.—Lankātilaka Vihāra, Polonnaruwa.

Sinhalese hold on Rāmēsvaram at least continued for some time, as Nissanka Malla claims to have built the Nissankēsvara temple there.

In A.B. 1708 (A.D. 1165/6) Parākrama was engaged in more peaceful pursuits, and with some trouble reconciled the three sects of priests, and purified the Buddhist religion ; the Vaitulya heresy now finally disappeared from Ceylon. Not content with this, the king built for the priesthood at Polonnaruwa the Jĕtavanārāma, including a round Tooth Relic temple, in the neighbourhood of the royal palace : further to the north he constructed the Ālāhana Parivēna (' Cremation College ') with the Lankātilaka Vihāra, until recently misnamed the ' Jĕtavanārāma ' ; as well as the Baddhasīmā Pāsāda, the so-called ' Priory.' Beyond this not far from the Mahā Thūpa (the real Demala Maha Sĕya, but now called Unagalā Vehera), he excavated the Uttarārāma or ' Northern Monastery,' the present Gal Vihāra ; while at the three branch cities or suburbs he erected the Isipatana, the Kusināra and the Vēluvana Vihāras. He also restored the shrines at Anurādhapura.

The king further enlarged and fortified Polonnaruwa, and adorned the city with numerous palaces and pleasure gardens. He also paid attention to irrigation, opening the Ākāsaganga (' Heavenly Ganges ') channel, the present Angamedilla Ela, from the Ambanganga, and forming or improving the ' Sea of Parākrama,' which included Tōpāvewa, as well as many other tanks throughout the country. Hereafter we hear nothing of irrigation : foreign disturbances, and, to a much greater degree, the appearance of malaria account for the collapse of the old works.

The internal peace of the kingdom seems only to have been disturbed by a rebellion in the neighbourhood of Mahātittha (Mantota) in Parākrama's sixteenth year (A.D. 1168/9). The king died after ruling thirty-three years, about A.D. 1186. His reign is considered to mark the zenith of Sinhalese greatness. Brilliant undoubtedly it was, but the constant wars, in particular that of the Pāndyan succession, and the numerous buildings impoverished the country, which never recovered. A few years after his death Nissanka Malla claims to have relieved the people from the heavy taxation imposed by his predecessor. A witness to the poverty of the time is the complete disappearance of the larger gold coinage. It is to be noted that Parākrama Bāhu, strong as he was, employed Tamil soldiers.

Parākrama was succeeded by his sister's son, Pandita Vijaya Bāhu, a learned man who himself wrote a Pāli letter to the king of Rāmañña. After a reign of one year he was killed in an intrigue with a cowherd's daughter by one, Mahinda, who was immediately put to death by Vijaya Bāhu's sub-king, Nissanka Malla.

Nissanka Malla (A.D. 1187-1196) ruled for nine years. He was born at Sinhapura in Kalinga in A.D. 1157/8, and was son-in-law or nephew to Parākrama Bāhu I., who brought him from his native country to Ceylon. He is the first of the pure Kalinga dynasty, and in his inscriptions which abound in Polonnaruwa is careful to inculcate the right of that family to the throne of Lankā, basing this claim on the ancestry of Vijaya, the first king. His documents are bombastic in the extreme, and he seems to have taken to himself the credit for many buildings erected by Parākrama Bāhu. He even claims to have reconciled the three sects of Buddhist priests, and to have invaded the Pāndyan country thrice. What is certain is that he built the Ruwanweli Dāgaba (the present Rankot Vehera) at Polonnaruwa, and also a new Tooth Relic temple, the construction of which is said to have taken sixty hours. He also embellished the cave temple of Dambulla. The Circular Relic House (Wata Dā-gē) attributed to him is really Parākrama's Tooth Relic shrine, converted by him

c.c.   E

to other purposes.   He was succeeded by his son Vīra
Bāhu, who only survived the night.

Fig. 17.—Kiri Vehera Dāgaba, Polonnaruwa.

A period of military rule now follows. The puppet
sovereigns set up often were of the Kalinga race. The

only one of real importance is Nissanka's half-brother
Sāhasa Malla, and this because the date of his coronation,
which took place on August 23, A.D. 1200, is the first
definitely fixed date in Ceylon history.   Anikanga, father
of the infant king Dharmāsōka, invaded Ceylon with an
army from the Chōla country, and slew his son and the
general who really governed, but he only held power for
seventeen days, when another general set up Parākrama
Bāhu's widow Līlāvatī.   She had already ruled in name
once before, and her second reign was interrupted by one
Lōkissara, who brought a Tamil host with him and held
Polonnaruwa for nine months.   The queen, now supported
by another general, again seized the throne, but was
speedily ousted by Parākrama Pāndya, perhaps a member
of the Pāndyan branch of the Sinhalese royal family, who
seems to have been a firm ruler.   The end was now at
hand, and after reigning three years he was deposed and
blinded about A.D. 1215 by Māgha, a scion of the Kalinga
race, who descended on Ceylon with a large army of
Kēralas or Malabars, doubtless claiming the kingdom by
inheritance through his kinsmen who had reigned before.
His rule might have been accepted by the people had
he not remained a bigoted Hindu and persecuted the
Buddhist faith, despoiling the temples and giving the lands
of the Sinhalese to his followers.   During the previous
anarchy the Tooth and Bowl Relics had been carried away
and hidden in Kotmalē, and the priests now scattered,
many going abroad to the Chōla and Pāndyan countries.
Māgha reigned twenty-one years (A.D. 1215-1236).

THE ADMINISTRATION.

With Parākrama Bāhu I. we once more gain an insight
into the government of the country.   While still only
ruler of the ʻ Southern Country,' he reorganized the

administrative system of his principality, and it is probable that he introduced the reforms then made into the government of the whole Island on his securing the crown. The sub-king's country before his time was ruled by two ministers, the ' Adigars of Lankā,' who, doubtless as in the last days of Kandyan rule, divided the supervision of the whole realm between them. Parākrama, with the object of obtaining a better revenue, separated ' all the land of great value,' in all probability the royal villages which in later days always contained the most fertile lands, and placed it under a third minister, perhaps the one known in the fourteenth century as the ' Adigar in charge of the palace.' We also hear of twelve governors of provinces, of eighty-four rulers of smaller districts, and of chiefs in charge of the borders, all with military and probably also with civil jurisdiction. The *Nikāya San-graha* attributes to Parākrama the creation or rather the reorganization of the great offices of State, as well as of the various departments, to which the villages throughout the kingdom were attached. It seems possible that he abolished the practical autonomy of the ' sub-king's country ' and of Ruhuna, establishing instead a centralized form of government for the whole Island.

In the last chapter we heard of the Council. Luckily the inscriptions on the pillars of Nissanka Malla's ' Council Chamber ' at Polonnaruwa supply us with definite information as to its constituent members. These were the Yuvaraja, otherwise known as Māpā, or sub-king ; the Ēpās or princes ; the Senevirad or commander-in-chief, often a member of the royal family ; the ' Principal Chiefs ' or Adigars, and the Chief Secretary with his subordinates, who all sat on the king's right hand ; on his left were the governors of provinces ; the chiefs of districts ; and the principal merchants, doubtless under their official head the Situ-nā. But we are still without knowledge as to the powers of this body.

The traditional ' fourfold army ' in India was composed of elephants, horses, chariots, and foot soldiers. In Ceylon in the period before the twelfth century we find the king in battle usually mounted on an elephant. His royal parasol was the rallying point of the army, and, as in South India, the king's flight or death entailed the rout of his host ; an instance of this is seen in the account of Kassapa I.'s defeat by his brother. Occasionally princes were mounted on horses, but these were always a luxury in the south, being imported at heavy cost. In the twelfth century there is no indication of the existence of organized units of elephants, chariots, or cavalry in Ceylon ; indeed the thickly wooded nature of

FIG. 18.—Sinhāsana Throne of Nissanka Malla.

the country, in which the operations took place, renders it very doubtful whether they could have been used to any extent. This is noteworthy, as during the Portuguese period in the low country elephants were employed in siege operations as well as in the van of the army. In the period under consideration a division consisted of infantry with the accompanying baggage train ; the generals were carried in palanquins and were distinguished by their parasols. The bulk of the troops presumably

then, as certainly in later days, consisted of local levies
and was stiffened by various select corps, such as the
'moonlight archers,' recruited for night work, and the
regiment of mace-bearers. These may be the 'eight
bodies of skilled foot soldiers,' said to have been organized
by Parākrama Bāhu I. In the opinion of foreigners the
efficiency of the troops was low, and Marco Polo (lib. iii.
cap. 14) states that in his day, at the end of the thirteenth century, the authorities employed 'Saracens' or
Muhammadan mercenaries. Under Parākrama Bāhu I.
the Ceylon records mention by name the Canarese, the
Kēralas, and the Tamils; the Vēlakkāra force had continued to exist since the days of Vijaya Bāhu I. In the
thirteenth century Rajputs are mentioned.

The offensive weapons in use were swords, spears, jave-
lins, and bows and arrows; the last-named sometimes
were poisoned. For defence the soldier employed a shield.
His armour in one passage of the *Mahāvansa* is stated to
have been of buffalo hide; that prepared for the expedition to Rāmañña is described as 'coats of iron and deer
skin.' In the fourteenth century the armour of the
Jaffna troops was 'many hued'; perhaps each regiment
had its distinctive colour.

Temporary fortresses played a great part in the civil
wars of the twelfth century. Such a stronghold consisted
of a stockade 'not to be shaken by elephants,' furnished
with a gate and surrounded by a ditch strewn with thorns;
the approaches through the surrounding forest were
blocked by barricades of trees. In one instance a gang
of housebreakers armed with sharp-edged deer horns was
dispatched to effect an entry into a fort of this kind. In
a stronghold of exceptional strength, described at length
in the *Mahāvansa*, a central tower of four stories was
surrounded by two concentric stockades, between which

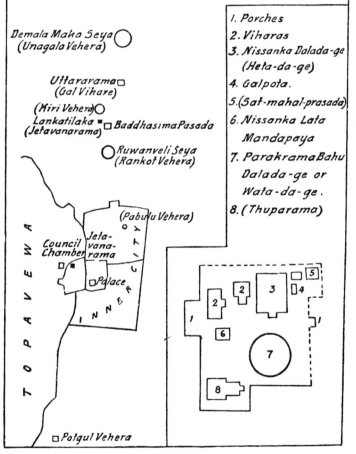

POLONNARUWA
with inset
showing
JETAVANARAMA AREA
(Modern names in brackets)

(Demala Maha Seya)

Demala Maha Seya
(Unagala Vehera)

Uttararama
(Gal Vihare)

(Kiri Vehera)
Lankatilaka
(Jetavanarama) Baddhasima Pasada

Ruwanveli Seya
(Rankot Vehera)

(Pabulu Vehera)

Jeta-
Council vana-
Chamber rama

Palace

INNER CITY

TOPAVEWA

Potgul Vehera

1. Porches
2. Viharas
3. Nissanka Dalada-ge
   (Heta-da-ge)
4. Galpota.
5. (Sat-mahal-prasada)
6. Nissanka Lata
   Mandapaya
7. Parakrama Bahu
   Dalada-ge or
   Wata-da-ge.
8. (Thuparama)

MAP IV.

lay a ditch twenty to thirty cubits wide, strewn with thorns and spikes. This ditch was some 700 feet round. Beyond the outer stockade lay another similar ditch, and beyond this a row of spikes and a thorn fence with a deeper ditch outside. The whole was surrounded by an open space cleared in the forest. The approaches were defended by concealed pits dug in the paths, commanded by archers in ambush. In the attack on this fortress we read of stones hurled from engines, of reeds fired and thrown among the enemy, and of fire-darts.

Permanent fortifications were to be found only in the case of cities. At Polonnaruwa in the twelfth century

FIG. 19.—Frieze, Vishnu Dēwālē, Polonnaruwa, No. 105.

and at Kurunēgala and Vātagiri in the thirteenth, we hear of ramparts, watch-towers, gates and gate-houses. In the next century Kōttē had its great moat and its ramparts with watch-towers, defended with spikes and calthrops. The Tamil soldiers, who came against this fortress, were provided with wicker screens as a protection against poisoned darts, and with mantlets, apparently for regular siege operations. Minor permanent defences were the watch-stations at strategic positions on the highways, usually at the boundary of a district. These simply consisted of a ' thorn-gate,' a movable screen hung on a door-frame, set in the path and sometimes furnished with wing-walls. These watch-stations or ' gravets ' continued in use until 1815.

AUTHORITIES FOR CHAPTER IV.

For general history see *Mhv.* and *Puj.*, and for the interregnum during the Chōla occupation, *S.I.I.* ii. No. 9 ; iii. i. Nos. 28, 29 ; *J.R.A.S.* 1913, pp. 519 ff.

Vijaya Bāhu I. The Ambagamuwa inscription (*E.Z.* ii. No. 35) makes his father to be King Abhā Salamevan ; it is probable that Moggallāna was nominal king, as an Abhā Salamevan is required between Mahinda V. (Siri Sanga Bō) and Vijaya Bāhu (also Siri Sanga Bō), and as Vikrama Bāhu refused the crown. If this be so Vijaya Bāhu's title of Yuvaraja is explained. Moggallāna may have died before his son's coronation. For Mahānāgakula on the Walawē see *Mānāvulu Sandēsaya* (*J.R.A.S.* 1905). For Vijayarājapura see the Vēlakkāra inscription (*A.S.*, 1911-12, p. 111 ; *J.R.A.S.*, *C.B.* xxix. No. 77, p. 266), and the Kapuru Vedu Oya record (*op. cit.*) ; the first mentioned record gives the king's age, the first *nakshatra* occurring on the actual day of his birth. The building of the Tooth Relic House at ' Kandavura,' *i.e.* Polonnaruwa, is recorded in the *Daladā Pūjāvaliya*.

Jaya Bāhu. See ' Dimbulāgala,' by H. C. P. Bell, *C.A.* x. pt. i. pp. 10 ff. For Tamil records of his reign see *A.S.* 1911-12, pp. 113 ff.

Parākrama Bāhu I. For the campaigns before his accession see "Notes on Ceylon Topography " (*op. cit.*). The irrigation works mentioned in *Mhv.* lxviii. are on the Deduru Oya and its neighbourhood, and not in Sabaragamuwa as supposed by Wijesinha. For Sugalā Dēvī's rebellion and the recovery of the Tooth Relic in the king's fourth year see *Daladā Pūjāvaliya* and *C.A.* ix. pt. iv. pp. 183 ff. ; the Tooth Relic, when in Ruhuna, was kept at Udundora Amaragiri, which is known from a Sinhalese verse to be the old name of Monarāgala ; the Pāli name Uruvēla of *Mhv.* lxxiv. and lxxix. is rendered in *Puj.* by ' Etumala-vewa,' the modern Etimolē. For Kusumiya see Hobson Jobson, *s.v.* Cosmin ; the grant to the successful general is given in the *Report on the Kēgalla District*, p. 75. For the war of the Pāndyan succession see the Chōla inscriptions, *A.R.E.* No. 20 of 1899, *ib.* 1899-1900, para. 38, *ib.* 1905-6, p. 70 ; *S.I.I.* iii. i. Nos. 86, 87, 88 ; *Ep. Ind.* vii. p. 169 ; for the Pallavarāyanpettai inscription relating Lankāpura's fate, dated 8 Rājādhirāja II. (1170-1), see *A.R.E.* 1924, No. 433. The Nissankēsvara temple is mentioned in *E.Z.* i. No. 9 ; ii. No. 17. The Convocation in A.B. 1708 is also recorded in *Daladā Pūjāvaliya.* As to Parākrama Bāhu's buildings at Polonnaruwa the arrangement in *Mhv.* lxxviii. is topographical, running from south to north. A similarly logical arrangement appears in chap. lxxix., vv. 14-60 dealing with the king's country, vv. 61-70 with the sub-king's country, and vv. 71-85 with Ruhuna. I identify the ' Sea of Parākrama ' with the chain of tanks along the Angamedilla Ela ; there still exist pillars on the embankments giving the length of Padi (Padawiya), Kanadiyadora (? Maha Kanadarāwa) and Kale (Kalāvewa) tanks, by which famous names the king designated those tanks of the chain. There was another ' Sea of Parākrama ' in the sub-king's country, made before Parākrama became king (*Mhv.* lxviii.). The name does not necessarily imply any great size, as the Kandy lake was known officially as the Kiri Muhuda or ' Sea of milk.'

The appearance of malaria may be referred to in Plancius' map of 1592, in which the following entry in Portuguese occurs : ' Kingdom of Jala deserted and depopulated for 300 years by reason of unhealthiness.' This ' kingdom ' is Yāla in the south-east of the Island.

Nissanka Malla. The date of his birth, A.B. 1700, is given in the Galpota inscription (*E.Z.* ii. No. 17). If this date can be interpreted as that of his arrival in Ceylon, the difficulty of his claim to have reconciled the priesthood, which took place in 1708, is removed. His claim of descent from Vijaya was due to the confusion of Sinhabāhu's capital with the Sinhapura in Kalinga and to the introduction of Kalinga into Vijaya's pedigree.

Sāhasa Malla. For the date of his accession see *E.Z.* ii.
No. 98, and Fleet, ' The Buddhavarsa,' *J.R.A.S.* 1909, p. 323.
For the chronology of the period see *C.A.* iv. pp. 33, 35, and
x. p. 98, and for the system of government *Mhv.* lxxix., *A.S.*
1900, p. 9 (*A.I.C.* 146), and *J.R.A.S.*, *C.B.* xxix. No. 77,
p. 304. On military matters the following references to the *Mhv.*
may be of use : xxxix. 25 ff. ; xliv. 19 ; l. 25 ; lxix ; lxx. 82,
100, 159, 168-169 ; lxxii. 266 ff. ; lxxiv. 32, 73 ; lxxv. 33 ;
lxxvi. 48. For the skilled foot soldiers see *N.S.* p. 20, where
it is mistranslated (viyat pat ata ganaya). In three passages
of the *Mhv.* a division is described as : sayogga-bala-vāhana.
A chariot is ratha. Vāhana in the case of the gods is a
' vehicle ' or rather a ' mount,' an animal. Here we may
translate : carts, men, and animals for use as mounts and for
transport. ' Yāna ' is translated by Wijesinha as ' chariot,'
' waggon ' in *Mhv.* lxx. 85, 122, but chap. xc. 5-8, distinctly
proves that the conveyance was a palanquin (andōli). As
to the coats (bānavāra) of iron and deer skin, the iron jackets
may have been of hide with iron plates or scales sewn on, or of
chain mail ; the name for this last (delu, Skt. jālaka) appears
in the fifteenth century *Ruwanmala*, which also mentions the
helmet. For the ' many hued ' armour see *N.S.* p. 26.

The great fort is described in *Mhv.* lxxii. 266 ff. For the
fortifications of Polonnaruwa see *Mhv.* lxx. 190 ; lxxiii. 57 ff. ;
for Kurunēgala and Vātagiri see *Puj.* (manuscript) ; for Kōttē,
N.S. p. 25. For the ' thorn-gates ' see the name Kantaka-
dvāra-vātaka in *Mhv.* lxxiv. 85 ; also Knox, bk. ii. chap. vi.
The word ' gravet ' comes through the Dutch from the Portuguese ' garaveto,' and this directly from the Sinhalese
' kadawata.'

CHAPTER V

THE DAMBADENIYA AND GAMPOLA KINGS,
1215-1411

WHILE the Kalinga Māgha was ruling at Polonnaruwa, a
Sinhalese prince Vijaya Bāhu III. (*c.* A.D. 1220-1224)
gradually gathered power into his hands, and succeeded in
expelling the foreigners from the Māyā country. The
contemporary records state that he was of the Siri Sanga
Bō family ; in greater detail he is said to have been the
son of Vijaya Malla, descended from the princes who
brought the Bo-tree. His son, however, in his poem the
Kavsilumina claims to be of the Lunar race descended
from King Pandu. Thus Vijaya Bāhu either was of the
Pāndyan branch of the royal family himself or more
probably married a princess of that race. From henceforth all the kings of the mediaeval period style themselves
Siri Sanga Bō.

The Sinhalese king, who had attained the sovereignty
well on in life, made his capital at Dambadeniya in
Kurunēgala District, and calling back the priests from
India conveyed the Tooth and Bowl Relics from their
hiding place in Kotmalē to the seat of government, and
thence to Beligala in Kēgalla District, where they were
lodged for the sake of safety. He also had the Scriptures
transcribed, and in addition built at the capital the Vijaya-
sundarārāma, so called after his own name, besides re-
pairing many temples. His convocation for the reform
of priestly discipline appears to have been held about
1222. He only reigned four years, and before his death
committed to the care of the priesthood his sons, Parākrama Bāhu and Bhuvanaika Bāhu, both of whom were

children. He was cremated at Attanagalla in Colombo District. The regnal years of Pandita Parākrama Bāhu II. (1234-1269), who was born at Sirivardhanapura not far from Dambadeniya, are reckoned in the contemporary *Pūjā-valiya* from about A.D. 1234, or some ten years after his father's death. A popular legend, which may have some foundation in fact, seems to assign to this period the usurpation of Prince Wattimi (Vathımi), the son of a king by a Muhammadan concubine. His rule was unpopular, and the chiefs having lured him to a high place at Kurunē-gala threw him over the precipice. His tomb, in the hands of the Muhammadans, is venerated also by the Sinhalese, to whom he is known as Galē Bandāra. The true heir, who was in hiding and who was traced by means of the state elephant, from the details given by the legend should be Parākrama Bāhu II. But the *Kurunēgala Vistaraya*, a work of no authority, while calling the heir Pandita Parākrama Bāhu of Dambadeniya, states that his father was Vanni Bhuvanaika Bāhu.

Parākrama Bāhu's coronation took place in 1236. His first act was to bring the Tooth Relic and lodge it at the capital. He then turned his attention to the recovery of Polonnaruwa from the Tamils, and achieved this purpose by 1244. In this connection two kings are mentioned, Māgha and Jaya Bāhu, who had been in power forty years, apparently reckoned from the time of the military rule after Sāhasa Malla. As the 'Tamil war' and the 'Malala war' are specifically mentioned by contemporary chronicles the two kings may have held different parts of the country. In the king's eleventh year (1244/5) Ceylon was invaded by Chandrabhānu, a Javanese (Jāvaka) from Tambalinga, with a host armed with blow-pipes and poisoned arrows : he may have been a sea-robber, and though now repulsed descended on the Island later on.

The rest of the reign according to the contemporary records was spent in pious works ; the king also held a convocation for the purpose of reforming the priesthood, whose discipline had been relaxed during the Tamil occupation. The chronicles make no mention of a great Pāndyan invasion which seems to have taken place between 1254 and 1256, in which one of the kings of Ceylon was slain and the other rendered tributary. From this it is clear that Parākrama Bāhu never had recovered the north of the Island, which certainly had been held by his great namesake.

After reigning thirty-three years he abdicated in favour of his eldest son Bosat Vijaya Bāhu IV. about A.D. 1267/8. The new king occupied himself in works of piety, and in completing the restoration of Polonnaruwa. Chandrabhānu again fell upon Ceylon with a mixed host of Pāndyans, Chōlas and Javanese, overran a considerable part of the north of the Island and encamped before Yāpahu, where he was defeated. The names Chāvakachchēri (" the Javanese settlement '), Chāvankōttai (' Javanese fort ') at Nāvatkuli in the Jaffna Peninsula, and Jāvakakōttē (' Javanese fort ') on the mainland possibly record settlements of his followers. Having attended to restorations at Anurādhapura, Vijaya Bāhu sent for his father to Polonnaruwa, where he was crowned a second time. The Tooth Relic having been brought, Parākrama held his ninth ordination festival at Dahastota, and then returned to Dambadeniya, where he died in his thirty-fifth year, probably in A.D. 1269 or early in 1270.

Vijaya Bāhu now was sole king, but was soon assassinated, possibly about October 1270, by his general, who assumed the crown. His younger brother, Bhuvanaika

Bāhu I. succeeded in escaping ; the usurper failing to
secure the allegiance of the Rajput mercenaries, who had
been won over by the true heir, was murdered, and the
prince crowned at the beginning of 1271. Early in his
reign he had to deal with a Pāndyan invasion, which he
repelled ; thereafter he lived for a few years at Dam-

Fig. 20.—Yāpahu.

badeniya, and then removed to Yāpahu. In the first
months of 1283 he dispatched an embassy to the Sultan of
Egypt proposing an alliance. As he reigned eleven years,
he must have died shortly afterwards. Hamir Sank, the
father of the ' Ceylon princess,' Pudmini, who married the
regent of Chitor about 1275, perhaps was one of the Rajput
mercenaries who took service in the Island.

The *Mahāvansa* relates that, apparently after Bhuvanaika Bāhu's death, there arose a famine and that the

Pāndyan king Kulasēkhara (A.D. 1268-1308) sent his minister Ārya Chakravarti to invade Ceylon. The minister, who is mentioned in a Pāndyan inscription of A.D. 1305, succeeded in taking Yāpahu, and in carrying off the Tooth Relic. But the *Daladā Sirita*, almost a contemporary document, places this event during Bhuvanaika Bāhu's reign, though doubtless it occurred at the very end of it. The chronicles represent Vijaya Bāhu's son, Parākrama Bāhu III. as immediately succeeding to the throne. But the Tamil poem *Sarajōti Mālai*, recited at his court in May A.D. 1310 was commenced in the seventh year from his coronation, and thus the reign must have begun about A.D. 1302 or 1303. This supposes a long interregnum of some twenty years, during which the Island perhaps formed part of the Pāndyan empire. It is at this time, between 1292 and 1294, that Marco Polo passed by Ceylon and mentions its king Sendemain, whose identity is obscure. An embassy also was sent in 1284 from China to secure the Tooth and Bowl Relics. Parākrama Bāhu had to humble himself by a personal embassy to the Pāndyan court, before he was able to get back the Tooth Relic : this he placed at Polonnaruwa, where he himself lived. The length of his reign is not known. Suspecting his cousin Bhuvanaika Bāhu, son of the king of that name, of conspiring to seize the throne, he sent his barber to blind him : the prince, however, fought and defeated the king, seized the Tooth Relic and removed it to his own city of Kurunēgala. It may be conjectured that Parākrama had secured the Relic at the price of vassalage to the Pāndyan court, and that the overthrow of that kingdom by the Muhammadans in 1310 was the occasion of his cousin's rebellion.

Vathimi Bhuvanaika Bāhu II. usually is said to have

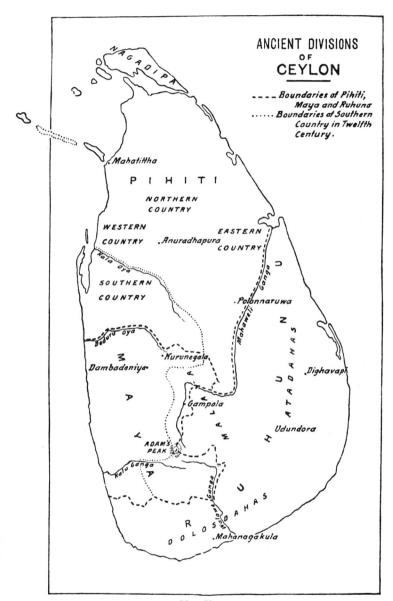

ANCIENT DIVISIONS
OF
CEYLON

- - - Boundaries of Pihiti,
Maya and Ruhuna
...... Boundaries of Southern
Country in Twelfth
Century.

NAGADIPA

Mahatittha

PIHITI

NORTHERN
COUNTRY

WESTERN
COUNTRY

EASTERN
COUNTRY

Anuradhapura

Kala Oya

SOUTHERN
COUNTRY

Polonnaruwa

Mahaweli Ganga

Deduru Oya

Kurunegala

MAYA

RUHUNA ATADAHAS

Dambadeniya

Dighavapi

Gampola

Udundora

ADAM'S
PEAK

Kalu Ganga

RUHUNA DOLOSDAHAS

Kalugamga

Mahanagakula

MAP V.

C.C.   F

died in his second year. This is due to a slight mislection in the received text of the *Mahāvansa*. The *Daladā Sirita*, composed in the next reign, assigns to him nine ordination festivals ; accordingly he must have reigned at least nine years.

His son, Parākrama Bāhu IV., came to the throne in the Saka year 1247 or A.D. 1325/6. He translated the Jātaka stories of Buddha's previous births into Sinhalese, built various temples, and in particular the Alutnuwara Dēwālē in Kēgalla District. The length of his reign is unknown, and the *Mahāvansa* chronicle ended with his death, until continued in the eighteenth century.

He was succeeded by Vanni Bhuvanaika Bāhu III. and Jaya or Vijaya Bāhu, of whom nothing is known. About the end of this last-named king's reign or the beginning of his successor's Ceylon was visited in 1344 by the famous traveller, Ibn Batuta, who found the north of the Island, including the port of Puttalam, in the possession of the king of Jaffna : the Sinhalese monarch he calls Alkonār, and states that he had been blinded in a palace revolution, but was still living while his son reigned in his stead. Colombo was then the seat of a Muhammadan pirate with an Abyssinian garrison. This city, which can be traced back as far as A.D. 949, is mentioned by a Chinese author in 1330. It has always been a foreign settlement. In the same year 1344 an inscription at Kelaniya records that the wife of the minister Alagak-kōnāra helped to repair the Kit Sirimevan Vihāra at that place. Ibn Batuta's ' Alkonār ' clearly is the same name ; the relationship with the royal family is obscure, but the queen of Parākrama Bāhu II. was of the Giri-vansa, to which clan belonged the great Alagakkōnāra, the all-powerful minister of Vikrama Bāhu III.

The capital, perhaps because of civil commotion, was

now moved to Gampola under Bhuvanaika Bāhu IV., who came to the throne in A.D. 1344/5 : the same date marks the accession of Parākrama Bāhu V., perhaps his brother. There were thus two sovereigns, a senior and a junior, at the same time, an arrangement which is found in the Chōla empire and with which we meet later in Ceylon.

FIG. 21.—Lankātilaka Vihāra, Kandy District.

The chief works of Bhuvanaika Bāhu's reign are the Lankātilaka and Gadalādeniya Vihāras, not far from Kandy. He ruled at least until 1353/4. Parākrama Bāhu V. is said to have reigned in Gampola, but the *Tisarā Sandēsaya* or ' Message of the Swan,' the earliest of this class of poem, is addressed to him at Dedigama in Kēgalla District : he may have resided here while Bhuvanaika Bāhu was at Gampola. His last known year is 1359. Joint king with him at least for a time was Vikrama Bāhu

III. (about 1357 to 1374 at least). It is in his reign that the great minister Alakēsvara or Alagakkōnāra came into prominence. Finding it expedient that the enemies of his country and religion should be kept at a distance the minister built the fortress of New Jayavardhanapura or Kōttē, not far from Colombo. Ārya Chakravarti, the king of Jaffna, attacked by sea and land, but was defeated, Alagakkōnāra capturing his encampments at Colombo, Wattala, Negombo and Chilaw. This campaign can hardly be other than that assigned by the *Rājāvaliya*, which at this period is very confused, to the reign of Bhuvanaika Bāhu V. According to this late chronicle the war was brought about by Alagakkōnāra hanging Ārya Chakravarti's tax collectors. It is unlikely that this is an invention. The very position of Kōttē in the swamps near Colombo is a proof of the straits to which the Sinhalese had been reduced, and there can be little doubt that the Jaffna kingdom was for a time paramount in the low country of Ceylon ; the Tamil inscription at Kotagama in Kēgalla District, however, is almost its only surviving relic. The attribution to Bhuvanaika Bāhu possibly may be due to a confusion between this campaign and the wars of Vīra Bāhu, his co-regent, vaguely referred to in the *Nikāya Sangraha*. In Vikrama Bāhu's time there took place in 1369/70 a reform of the priesthood, which lasted until the fifteenth year of the next reign.

Bhuvanaika Bāhu V. (A.D. 1372/3 to 1406/7 at least), reigned in Gampola : he seems to have been little more than a figure-head. A Vijayanagar record of A.D. 1385/6 relates that the prince, Virūpāksha, conquered among others the Sinhalas, and presented crystals and other jewels to his father Harihara ; this may refer to the kingdom of Jaffna, which in the next century was tributary to the great empire on the mainland. The fifteenth year of Bhuvanaika Bāhu fell in A.B. 1929 or A.D. 1386/7, and in his twentieth (A.D. 1391/2) the sub-king Vīra Bāhu, his cousin and brother-in-law, came to the throne. The documents, however, prove that Bhuvanaika Bāhu continued to reign, in name if not in fact, for some fifteen years longer. Before Vīra Bāhu's accession, however, the actual royal authority had been wielded by Kumāra Alakēsvara, the son of the great Alagakkōnāra, who had died after 1382/3, and then by Vīra Alakēsvara. With him fought his brother Vīra Bāhu II., who resided at Rayigampura in Kalutara District, and Vīra Alakēsvara fled to India. Vīra Bāhu had to deal with hostile designs on the part of Tamils, Moors and others ; he was pious, and held another convocation for the reform of the priesthood in A.B. 1939 or A.D. 1396/7. He was succeeded by his two sons, whose reigns must have been very short, as Vīra Alakēsvara returned from India, seized the supreme power, and reigned for twelve years, apparently under the name of Vijaya Bāhu VI. According to the Chinese authorities he was a ' Suoli,' as was Parākrama Bāhu VI., that is, not a Chōla as has been supposed, but one of the Savulu or Sākya race, for these Alakēsvaras were members of the Sinhalese royal family, being of the Mehenavara clan on the one side and of the Ganavesi on the other. Vijaya Bāhu had the misfortune to deal unfairly with a Chinese mission, and the ambassador Ching Ho retaliated by carrying off the king with his wives and children, returning to China in A.D. 1411. The emperor ordering the captive's family to chose a successor, they selected the Ēpā, who was sent back to Ceylon with the deposed king. The prince so chosen does not seem to be the Parākrama Bāhu Ēpā, the successor of Vijaya Bāhu, and grandson of Sēnālankādhikāra Senevirat, minister of Bhuvanaika

Bāhu IV. This Parākrama was followed by Parākrama
Bāhu ,VI. An inscription in Chinese, Persian and Tamil,
dated in A.D. 1409, found at Galle, refers to Ching Ho's
expedition. The reputation enjoyed by Parākrama Bāhu II. is due
to the religious and literary activities of his reign. He
recovered the two old capitals from the foreigner, but
never succeeded in ousting him from the extreme north,
nor do we know that he ever attempted to do so. It is
at this period that we hear of the Vanniyars, to whom
the safety of Anurādhapura was entrusted. These chiefs
in later days occupied the frontier country between Jaffna
and the Sinhalese kingdom, and were subjects of one or
other of these states, or affected complete independence
according to the strength of their neighbours. The reign,
which had begun so well, ended in weakness, and Parākrama set the fatal example of dividing his kingdom among
his sons and nephew, piously enjoining them to live at
peace with one another. This policy later on was to be
the direct cause of European settlement in the Island.
The weakness of the government also is disclosed by the
failure of Vijaya Bāhu IV. to enforce the payment of
taxes, and his custom of supplying the deficiency from
the royal treasury. The mutiny, which cost him his life,
probably may be attributed to his inability to pay his
mercenary troops.

The whole period indeed is one of slow decline. The
Lankātilaka and Gadalādeniya temples, already mentioned,
are the only buildings of note, and Dambadeniya, Kurunēgala, and Gampola are in marked contrast to Polonnaruwa in the absence of structural remains. Even the
Tooth Relic temple erected by Parākrama Bāhu II. in his
early years had to be rebuilt before the end of the reign.
An incontrovertible sign of national poverty is the fact,

attested by a contemporary work, that by the time of Parākrama Bāhu IV. the ' gold massa ' had become a copper coin. There are indications that the removal of the seat of government to Gampola was due to internal trouble : the palace revolution recorded by Ibn Batuta has been noted, and tradition attributes the abandonment of Kurunēgala by Parākrama Bāhu V. to war. We have also observed the great extension of the power of Jaffna in the second and third quarters of the fourteenth century. We shall see that the decline of the Sinhalese monarchy was arrested for the time by Parākrama Bāhu VI.

AUTHORITIES FOR CHAPTER V

For general history see *Mhv.* (of little value after the reign of Parākrama Bāhu IV.) ; *Puj.*, especially the unpublished longer version, and *Hatthavanagalla Vihāra-vansa*, both contemporary with Parākrama Bāhu II. ; the *N.S.*, composed at the end of the fourteenth century, and its derivative and continuation the *Saddh.* For the Dambadeniya period see ' Notes on the Dambadeniya Dynasty,' *C.A.* x. pt. i. pp. 37 ff. and pt. ii. pp. 88 ff.

Parākrama Bāhu II. For the Pāndyan invasion see *A.R.E.* inscriptions Nos. 421 of 1907, 356 of 1906, and also volume for 1912, p. 65. For Jāvakakōttē, situated between Māvatupatuna (Mantota) and Kalmunai, see *Kokila Sandēsaya,* v. 236.

Bhuvanaika Bāhu I. The Pāndyan incursion seems to be referred to in *A.R.E.* No. 698 of 1916. For the Rajputs in Ceylon see Tod, *Annals of Rajasthan,* i. p. 276, and *C.A.* x. p. 88 ; their chief was called Thakuraka, a well-known Rajput title. For the embassy to Egypt see *J.R.A.S., C.B.* xxviii. No. 72, p. 82. The inscription referring to Ārya Chakravarti is *A.R.E.* No. 110 of 1903.

Parākrama Bāhu III. The *Sarajōti Mālai* is published at the Kokuvil Press, Jaffna, 1910 (second edition). For the conspiracy of Bhuvanaika Bāhu see Wijesinha's *Mhv.* p. 316, and Upham's *Mhv. (Sacred and Historical Books of Ceylon,* 1833, vol. i. p. 355). Civil war is definitely mentioned in the *Daladā Sirita,* written under Parākrama Bāhu IV. *Bhuvanaika Bāhu II.* For the mislection see *C.A.* x. pt. ii. p. 91. *Parākrama Bāhu IV.* The date of accession appears in the contemporary *Daladā Sirita.* For Alutnuwara Dēwālē see *C.A. ib.* p. 92. Tradition assigns the foundation to Bhuvanaika Bāhu I. (Lewukē Sannasa, *Report on the Kēgalla District,* p. 47).

The work of Ibn Batuta as far as it touches Ceylon has been translated in *J.R.A.S., C.B.* 1882 ; for ' Alkonār' see *ib.* xxix. No. 75, p. 106. The Muhammadan tombstone at Colombo, giving the Hijra year 337 (A.D. 949), is published in *Transactions R.A.S.* i. 545. For the Chinese book *Tao I Chih Lüeh* see *J.R.A.S., C.B.* xxviii. No. 73. For the Kit Sirimevan inscription see *C.A.* i. p. 152 ; ii. pp. 149, 182. For the Giri-vansa see D. B. Jayatilaka's ' Daily Routine of Parākrama Bāhu' in the *Buddhist,* July 8, 1922.

According to Chau Ju-Kua's work on the Chinese and Arab trade in the twelfth and thirteenth centuries (F. Hirth and W. W. Rockhill, St. Petersburg, 1912), Si-lan was under the rule of Nan-p'i or Malabar and sent a yearly tribute to San-fo-ts'i (Palembang in Sumatra). The first statement perhaps refers to Māgha and his Kēralas ; the second may furnish a clue to Tambalinga, the home of Chandrabhānu. There is a Tambilang river on the east coast of Sumatra.

For the cause of the abandonment of Kurunēgala see under Parākrama Bāhu V.

Bhuvanaika Bāhu IV. The date of accession is given in the Lankātilaka (*J.R.A.S., C.B.* x. No. 34, pp. 83 ff.) and Gadalādeniya inscriptions as Saka 1266. The date A.B. 1894 = A.D. 1351/2 for his fourth year expired appears in *N.S.,* which is wrong also in two other dates (*C.A.* ix. p. 186).

Parākrama Bāhu V. For the war which caused him to leave Kurunēgala see Lawrie's *Gazetteer,* vol. ii. p. 581, and *C.A.*

x. p. 97. The date of accession is given in the Hapugastenna inscription (*J.R.A.S.*, *C.B.* xxii. No. 65, p. 362).

Vikrama Bāhu III. For date of accession see Vigulawatta inscription in *Report on the Kēgalla District*, p. 79, and for the last known year the Niyangampāya record in *J.R.A.S.*, *C.B.* xxii. No. 65, p. 343. For the war with Jaffna I have followed the slightly later *N.S.* rather than the more modern and confused *Raj.*, which, however, contains valuable details. The Kotagama inscription is published in the *Report of the Kēgalla District*, p. 85 ; but the translation has to be amended, ' Sētu ' being the motto of the Jaffna kings and ' Anurēsar ' meaning ' Lord of Anurai,' a word used in Tamil originally for Anurādhapura, and then for any capital of the Sinhalese.

Bhuvanaika Bāhu V. For the Virūpāksha inscription see *Ep. Ind.* iii. No. 32. For the date of accession see *N.S.*, and for the thirty-fourth or thirty-sixth year, *J.R.A.S.*, *C.B.* xxii. No. 65, p. 366. The last mention of the great Alagakkōnāra is in Saka 1304 (1382/3) in the Sinhalese Attanagalu-vansa. The ' prabhurāja ' of the *Mayūrā Sandēsaya* is Vīra Alakēsvara, brother of Vīra Bāhu and brother-in-law of Bhuvanaika Bāhu V.

For the successors of Bhuvanaika Bāhu V. see *Saddh.* p. 295, a nearly contemporary work. For *Vijaya Bāhu VI.* see the controversy in *J.R.A.S.*, *C.B.* xxii. No. 65, pp. 316 ff. Kēragala inscription No. 1, referring to 11 Vijaya Bāhu, in reality is a schedule to inscription No. 2, but Mr. H. C. P. Bell's contention that Vijaya Bāhu reigned shortly before Parākrama Bāhu VI. is not affected thereby as the sister of Alagakkōnāra is mentioned in No. 1. The royal descent of the later Alakēsvaras is given in the Sagama inscription (*J.R.A.S.*, *C.B. ib.* p. 364). For the Chinese authorities see *ib.* xxiv. No. 68, pp. 74 ff. and xxviii. No. 73, p. 32, and for the trilingual record *Spolia Zeylanica*, viii. pt. xxx. 1912. The proof that Parākrama Bāhu Ēpā is not identical with Parākrama Bāhu VI. is found in the numeration of the kings in *Saddh.* p. 71, where however ' 116 ' in line 3 should read ' 115 ' (*pasalos* for *solos*).

For the building and restoration of Parākrama Bāhu II.'s
Tooth Relic temple see *Mhv.* lxxxii. 8 ; lxxxv. 91 ; and *Puj.*
The reference to the copper ' masuran ' coins is in the Sinhalese
Ummagga Jātaka ; see version by T. B. Yatawara, London,
1898, p. 158, line 31, where, however, ' gold ' should be ' coin.'

CHAPTER VI

THE KŌTTĒ DYNASTY AND ITS PORTUGUESE ALLIES
1412-1550

PARĀKRAMA BĀHU VI. (A.D. 1412-1468) is said to have
been the son of Vijaya Bāhu VI. and his queen Sunētra
Dēvī of the Kalinga race ; this paternity, however, is
disputed by some scholars. The constant tradition is
that his mother and her two sons escaped when Vijaya
Bāhu was carried off by the Chinese, and remained in
hiding at Rukulēgama in Kēgalla District for fear of an
Alakēsvara who had been left as regent, and that finally
the elder prince killed this Alakēsvara and ascended the
throne. The story is intelligible if, as seems possible,
Parākrama Bāhu Ēpā was an Alakēsvara who seized
power on the removal of Vijaya Bāhu and was not the
same as the prince selected in China : indeed, Do Couto,
who had access to manuscripts in the possession of Sinhalese princes at Goa, asserts that the king on his return
to Ceylon was murdered by this Alakēsvara. The younger
of the two brothers was the sub-king Māyādunne Parākrama Bāhu.

The date of Parākrama Bāhu VI.'s accession also is in
dispute. Some contemporary writers place it in A.B. 1955
(A.D. 1412/3) ; official documents, however, usually date
his regnal years from A.B. 1958 (A.D. 1415/6). As the king
is said to have lived for three years at Rayigam-pura and

then to have gone to Kōttē, where he was crowned, it seems probable that he came to the throne in A.D. 1412 and was inaugurated in 1415. One contemporary work dates the reign from A.B. 1953, but in another passage from A.B. 1958 ; as it equates the latter year with the year 1722 from the conversion of Ceylon to Buddhism it is preferable to accept this date as correct and to treat 1953 as a clerical error.

Relations with China still continued, and tribute was sent in 1436, in 1445, and for the last time in 1459.

Parākrama Bāhu's religious works included the building of a temple for the Tooth Relic at Kōttē, and of the Pepiliyāna Vihāra near Colombo in honour of his mother ; he also restored the Saman Dēwālē near Ratnapura, founded in the time of Parākrama Bāhu II., and endowed the Aramanapola Vihāra not far from Pelmadulla, the architecture of which is noteworthy.

The sequence of events in this reign is far from clear. The principal event was the conquest of Jaffna by Sapumal Kumārayā, the son, actual or adopted, of Parākrama Bāhu. This kingdom seems to have come into being, at least as an independent state, about the thirteenth century. The place-names in the peninsula indicate that it was held by Sinhalese inhabitants at no very remote date, and it certainly was part of the dominions of Parākrama Bāhu I. Its sovereigns, the Ārya Chakravartis, were of mixed descent, claiming to be of the Ganga-vansa, the ruling race of Kalinga, and to be Brahmans from Rāmēsvaram. The most probable solution of the problem is that the Kalinga Māgha or his heirs never lost their hold on the Jaffna peninsula, in which at least two of their forts, Ūrātota (Kayts) and Veligama (Vālikāmam, perhaps Kānkēsanturai), were situated, and that, as stated by De Queyroz, one of the Ārya Chakravartis, a well-known family in the

Pāndyan country, married a daughter of the then king. In 1344 the king of Jaffna held a considerable part of the north of Ceylon, and the last half of the fourteenth century marked the zenith of his power : we have seen that for a short time the overlordship of the Island was in his hands. By the beginning of the next century, if not at the end of the preceding, the kingdom was tributary to the great continental empire of Vijayanagar. Nunez states this definitely, and one of the regular titles of the emperor was " who levied taxes from Ĩlam ' ; the Sinhalese poems of

FIG. 22.—Jaffna Coin.

the time also constantly speak of the people of Jaffna as Canarese. Valentyn mentions an invasion of the Canarese, that is of the Vijayanagar forces ; it is uncertain whether this was the occasion or the result of the conquest of Jaffna. What is clear is that Sapumal Kumārayā conquered the northern kingdom, advancing along the west coast road. The reduction of the Vanni may have preceded this event. Apparently connected with the campaign was the expedition to Adriampet in South India, occasioned according to Valentyn by the seizure of a Ceylon ship laden with cinnamon. The conquest of Jaffna is already mentioned in the thirty-sixth year of the reign, that is either A.D. 1447/8 or 1450/1. The Tenkāsi inscription of Arikēsari Parākrama Pāndya of Tinnevelly, ' who saw the backs of kings at Singai, Anurai,' and elsewhere, may refer to these wars, Singai being the Jaffna capital and Anurai the Sinhalese ; it is dated between A.D. 1449/50 and 1453/4.

According to the *Rājāvaliya* the king had reigned for fifty-two years when Jotiya Sitāno, the ruler of the hill-

country, revolted. The rebel was deposed, and a prince
of the Gampola royal family set up in his stead. Valentyn
places this event between the Adriampet expedition and
the reduction of the Vanni previous to the conquest of
Jaffna. Jotiya appears as a witness to the Madawala
inscription in Dumbara dated in the seventeenth year of
the reign (A.D. 1428/9 or 1431/2).

Parākrama Bāhu abdicated in favour of his daughter's
son, Vīra Parākrama Bāhu, and died after a reign of fifty-
five or fifty-two years, according as this is reckoned as
beginning in 1412 or 1415. His reign is noted for a great
outburst of Sinhalese literature, in particular of poetry.
The king raised the nation to a height never attained since
the days of Parākrama Bāhu II., and never afterwards
rivalled.

Vīra Parākrama Bāhu or Jaya Bāhu (1468-c. 1470) is
said by the *Rājāvaliya* to have been slain by Sapumal
Kumārayā, who hearing of his accession hurried from
Jaffna. Do Couto, however, who was well-informed, says
that when this king had ruled one and a half years his
uncle Māyādunnē Parākrama Bāhu died and was succeeded by Sapumal Kumārayā's brother, usually known
as Ambulugala Raja from the name of his seat in Kēgalla
District. After a few years' reign the king died and his
half-witted son was put on the throne by his aunt, who
two years later finding herself unable to rule sent for
Sapumal Kumārayā from Jaffna.

This prince ascended the throne under the name of
Bhuvanaika Bāhu VI. (c. A.D. 1472-1480 at least) and was
crowned in A.B. 2015. An embassy arrived from Pegu for
the purpose of obtaining the priestly succession from
Ceylon in 1476, at a moment when a serious rebellion had
broken out. In the chronicles this king is given a reign
of seven years from his coronation, but the Dedigama

inscription is dated in his ninth year.   He was succeeded by his son Pandita Parākrama Bāhu VII., who was attacked and slain by his uncle Ambulugala Raja : Do Couto states that he reigned for not more than four years.   Ambulugala Raja assumed the name of Vīra Parākrama Bāhu VIII.   He is given a reign of twenty years in the *Rājāvaliya*, but it is difficult to accept this figure ; he probably ruled as sole king from about 1484 to 1509.   He had several sons, and the difficulties in the chronology of the time are largely due to contemporaneous reigns.

On November 15, 1505, the Island was first visited by Dom Lourenço de Almeida, who set up the usual padrão at Colombo : this, a rock carved with the arms of Portugal, was in the Customs premises until removed to the Gordon Gardens at the side of Queen's House.   The Portuguese made a great impression on the inhabitants of Colombo, and according to the *Rājāvaliya* their report to the king ran thus : " There is in our harbour of Colombo a race of people fair of skin and comely withal.   They don jackets of iron and hats of iron : they rest not a minute in one place : they walk here and there ; they eat hunks of stone and drink blood ; they give two or three pieces of gold and silver for one fish or one lime ; the report of their cannon is louder than thunder when it bursts upon the rock Yugandhara.   Their cannon balls fly many a gawwa and shatter fortresses of granite.'   The Portuguese envoys were conducted to the court by a circuitous way, by which they took three days to reach Kōttē, lying only six miles from Colombo : this has passed into a proverb in Sinhalese, though the Portuguese were not taken in by the trick.   In spite of the intrigues of the Muhammadans, the so-called Moors, who had most to lose by the arrival of the foreigners, Dom Lourenço took the king under the protection of Portugal, with a promise of cinnamon as tribute.

Parākrama Bāhu had constant trouble with his relatives ; civil war was the besetting sin of the dynasty and led to its downfall. In the later months of 1508 he had been very ill, and as Dharma Parākrama Bāhu IX. and his

FIG. 23.—The Portuguese Padrão, Colombo.

brother Vijaya Bāhu VII. both reckon their reigns from 1509, it would appear that he made his sons co-regents with him in that year. In 1513 the king was reported to be dead, leaving his two sons quarrelling over the succession ; but it is stated by De Queyroz that in 1518 he was an old man with a white beard, and that Vijaya Bāhu, impatient of his father's prolonged life and incapacity to rule, dethroned and subsequently poisoned him. Though he must have been about eighty at his death, it seems likely that his reign actually extended till 1518, when Parākrama Bāhu IX. (A.D. 1509-1528 at least) succeeded as senior king. This monarch was of little importance, as he is omitted altogether by certain chronicles, and Vijaya Bāhu, whose first grant issued at Kōttē is dated in 1519/20, and his successors apparently ignored his existence. He is given a reign of twenty or twenty-two years in the *Rājāvaliya*, and perhaps spent his last years at Kelaniya.

In 1518, as we have seen, Vijaya Bāhu VII. (A.D. 1509-1521) seized the government, and, instigated by the Moors, lost no time in sending to the Samorin of Calicut, the suzerain of Malabar, then at war with Portugal, for help to enable him to attack the Portuguese fort of Colombo, which had been erected shortly before. The Sinhalese were beaten off, and the king, losing prestige in the war that ensued, ultimately lost his throne and his life in the ' Sacking of Vijaya Bāhu ' in 1521, at the hands of the sons of himself and his brother Rājasinha by a common wife, the eldest of whom became king as Bhuvanaika Bāhu VII. (A.D. 1521-1550). According to other accounts Vijaya Bāhu's fall was due to his intention of disinheriting the sons in favour of a young prince whom he had adopted. The fort was demolished on orders from Portugal in 1524, though a factor was still left in charge of Portuguese interests.

In 1521 the country had been divided between the three brothers, Māyādunnē taking practically the modern Province of Sabaragamuwa, with his capital at Sītāwaka (Avissāwēlla), while Rayigam Bandāra received the Walallāwiti, Pasdun, and Rayigam Korales in the Galle and Kalutara Districts, the seaports being reserved to Bhuvanaika Bāhu. The hill-country was in the hands of another king, who asserted complete independence whenever possible. Māyādunnē aspired to the throne of Kōttē and the overlordship of the Island, and in the years following 1526 an almost continual conflict was waged between himself, aided by the Samorin on the one hand, and Bhuvanaika Bāhu supported by the Portuguese on the other. In 1539, however, Māyādunnē was forced to make peace, which lasted until 1547.

About 1538 Bhuvanaika Bāhu's daughter had been married to one Vīdiyē Bandāra, and, with the object of making his position more secure against Māyādunnē, an embassy was dispatched in 1540 to Lisbon with a golden image of their infant son Dharmapāla, requesting that the prince should be installed by the king of Portugal as the heir apparent of the kingdom of Kōttē. This was duly done, and with the ambassadors on their return journey came the first Franciscans, whose missionary zeal showed itself first at Kōttē and shortly afterwards in Kandy. In 1547 the war was renewed by Māyādunnē, but he was compelled to retire to Deraniyagala, leaving his chief city to the king of Kōttē and the Portuguese. Expeditions by the Portuguese in the hill-country, which we may now call the kingdom of Kandy, led to two severe disasters : Māyādunnē sowed dissension between Bhuvanaika Bāhu and his Portuguese allies, and the war was still in progress, when in 1550 the new Viceroy Dom Affonco de Noronha unexpectedly arrived in Colombo, having been driven out of his course on his way to Goa. This dignitary suspected Bhuvanaika Bāhu's good faith and proceeded to quarrel with him. But the old king showed some spirit and ordered the Viceroy out of his kingdom. He left, but the king's days were numbered, and on December 29, 1550, he was shot while looking out of a window in his palace at Kelaniya. There were good grounds for suspecting that it was done at the Viceroy's

c.c. G

orders. The people so believed, and in their fury razed the factory. The death of Bhuvanaika Bāhu proved disastrous to the Portuguese, as within a few years the kingdom of Kōttē practically was confined to the capital and its neighbourhood : Māyādunnē was the real sovereign. Thus ended the first phase of the Portuguese connection with Ceylon. At first trade was their chief concern and the establishment was a factory or trading-station under a factor. The civil strife between the king of Kōttē and his brother drove the former into close alliance with Portugal and led to the frequent presence of Portuguese troops. In the second phase the fortress of Colombo with its captain and garrison, maintained for the protection of Dharmapāla of Kōttē, comes into prominence ; the hostility of Māyādunnē and his son rendered the new king more and more dependent on foreign help. The third and last phase began when the Portuguese, heirs designate of Kōttē, on the crumbling of the Sītāwaka realm, annexed the rival capital without trouble and then embarked on a career of conquest. The chief official of this period is the ' Captain General of the Conquest.'

The account of the political divisions of Ceylon presented by the schedule attached to Dharmapāla's Donation must refer to a period long anterior to 1580, the date of the execution of this document, and so may find a place in this chapter. The states over which the king of Kōttē claimed suzerainty were the kingdoms of Sītāwaka, of the (Seven) Kōralēs, of Candea or the hill-country, and of Jaffna, and also the principality of the Four Kōralēs. There also were various Vanniyarships, who were bound by tribute to the king of Kōttē. These were the two Pānamas ; Yāla ; ' Velewara Kosgamma ' ; Wellassa ; Palugama ; Batticaloa ; Kottiyar ; Trincomalee ; and Puttalam. This last and Yāla were held by several

Vanniyars, Palugama by two, the others by one each.
In the kingdom of Kōttē itself were three Disāwas, one
over Mātara, one over the Adikāriya of Denawaka with
the Āgras or gem-pits of Sabaragamuwa, and one over
the Adikāriya of Nuwarakalāwiya, the country forming the
western half of the present North Central Province and
stretching according to our document from Puttalam
to Mannar. Apart from this last Adikāriya or jurisdiction, the immediate possessions of Kōttē are given
as 22½ kōralēs, which included the south-west corner of
the North-Western Province, with a small exception the
whole of the Western and Southern Provinces as far as
the Walawē River, and that part of the Ratnapura
District to the south of the Kalu-ganga with the great
villages Gilīmalē and Bambarabotuwa. The small exception referred to is the half of Hēwāgam Kōrale, which
belonged to Sītāwaka.

AUTHORITIES FOR CHAPTER VI

For general history see *Raj.* and the version of the same
preserved in Valentyn, *Oud en Nieuw Oost Indien*, vol. v. ;
extracts from Do Couto and De Barros by Donald Ferguson,
J.R.A.S., C.B. xx. No. 60 ; De Queyroz, *Conquista Temporal
e Espiritual de Ceylão*, Government Press, 1916 ; P. E. Pieris,
Ceylon : the Portuguese Era, Colombo, 1913, written from the
Sinhalese standpoint.

Parākrama Bāhu VI. For his paternity see ' Vijaya Bāhu
VI.', *J.R.A.S., C.B.* xxii. No. 65, pp. 316 ff. ; in the *Rājā-
vansaya* (Colombo Museum MS.) Vīra Bāhu is called Vijaya
Bāhu, and in a manuscript collection of notes on various
dates Vīra Bāhu is given as the father of Parākrama Bāhu VI.,
but both works are modern. The sub-king is mentioned in
the *Paravi Sandēsaya.*
The date of accession, A.B. 1953, appears in *Saddh.* p. 71,

and the date, A.B. 1958, on p. 295. For the tribute to China see *J.R.A.S.*, *C.B.* xxiv. No. 68, p. 111. The Pepiliyāna inscription has been published *ib.* vii. No. 25, p. 187, but a number of documents connected with it and including the Aramanapola grant are in manuscript and have not been published ; from the internal evidence they are genuine. The Saman Dēwālē grant has been edited in *C.A.* ii. p. 43. For Sinhalese place names in the Jaffna peninsula see *C.A.* ii. pp. 54, 167 ff. The occupation of the north by Parākrama Bāhu I. is evidenced by the unpublished Nayinativu inscription. For the descent of the Jaffna kings see Rev. S. Gnana Prakasar, *C.A.* v. pt. iv. pp. 172 ff., and *De Q.* pp. 37, 38. The date 1344 is that of Ibn Batuta's visit. For the Vijayanagar suzerainty see *J.R.A.S.*, *C.B.* (Notes and Queries), xxvi. No. 70, pt. ii. p. 101, and Nunez in Sewell, *A Forgotten Empire*, London, 1900. For the Tenkāsi inscription see *Travancore Archaeological Series*, vi. No. 11.

Bhuvanaika Bāhu VI. The date, A.B. 2015, in the *Budugunālankāraya*, judging from the usage in other documents, refers to the king's accession and not to his third year. For the Kalyāni inscription see *J.R.A.S.*, *C.B.* xxiii. No. 67, pp. 231 ff., and for the Dedigama record the *Report on the Kēgalla District*, p. 83.

Parākrama Bāhu VIII. His illness in 1508 is referred to in De Barros, ii., iii. 1 (*J.R.A.S.*, *C.B.*, xix. No. 59, p. 366), and his death reported in 1513 in a letter of D'Albuquerque to the king, *Alguns Documentos*, p. 297. The presentation of his reign in the text seems to me to be the most probable, unless a generation has been dropped as perhaps may be deduced from *De Q.*, p. 20. Valentyn (p. 74), speaking of Vīra Parākrama Bāhu, the grandson of Parākrama Bāhu VI., states that Ambulugala Raja was his mother's sister's son. The *Raj.* has confused Ambulugala Raja to some extent with Māyādunnē Parākrama Bāhu, who held the same principality ; according to Do Couto the last named prince survived Parākrama Bāhu VI.

Parākrama Bāhu IX. For the Kelaniya inscription see *C.A.* i. p. 155.

Vijaya Bāhu VII. His grants are : fourth year for Dondra, ninth year from Udugampola, eleventh year from Kōttē. The Udugampola sannasa was granted on the occasion of an eclipse of the sun. Such eclipses occurred on the required date in 1517 and 1518, but the second is said not to have been visible in Ceylon. The accession, therefore, took place in 1509, and the Saka year 1432 of the Dondra grant must be 'current.'

Bhuvanaika Bāhu VII. See *J.R.A.S., C.B.* xxii. No. 65, pp. 267 ff. For records of the kings of the Hill Country see *Report on the Kēgalla District,* pp. 80, 81, wrongly attributed to Vikrama Bāhu III. ; other unpublished inscriptions of Jayavīra Parākrama Bāhu exist at Gadalādeniya.

The Donation of Dharmapāla with the connected documents is given in *De Q.* pp. 428, 429, and in the *Orientalist,* iii. pp. 111, 131, 193. The Denawaka Adikāriya perhaps equals the Denawaka pas rata of the Kadaim-pota ; in the list of kōralēs 'Attalagam' can hardly be Atulugam, which is too near Sītāwaka, and must represent Atakalan, while 'Tarana' may be Etarawā, now in Uva but once belonging to Sabaragamuwa.

CHAPTER VII

THE ASCENDENCY OF SĪTĀWAKA AND OF PORTUGAL
1550-1635

THE young Dharmapāla (1550-1597) now was set on the throne of Kōttē by his father Vīdiyē Bandāra. News of his grandfather's death and of the destruction of the factory reached Goa, and the Viceroy hastened to Colombo, more with a view to extortion than to assisting the new ruler. The unfortunate king and his courtiers were robbed of their valuables, and the palace and city systematically plundered. This scandalous action, the more abominable as the victim was under the protection of Portugal, met with strong disapproval at home ; restitution was ordered, but with the law's delays little of the stolen property ever was recovered by the owners. The Viceroy next set out with Dharmapāla for Sītāwaka, where he sacked the temple, Berendikōvil, the remains of which still exist, but refused to press matters to a conclusion with Māyādunnē, when he had the opportunity. The subsequent destruction of Kōttē and the loss of the kingdom in a large degree is due to this man. He then sailed from Colombo, leaving secret instructions for the kidnapping of the king's father. This was carried out in 1552, but Vīdiyē Bandāra succeeded in escaping from his prison, and henceforth was the bitter enemy of the Portuguese. At first he allied himself with Māyādunnē, whose daughter he married, but soon was the object of attack at his fortress of Pelenda in Kalutara District both by Rājasinha, son of Māyādunnē, and by the Portuguese. Rājasinha is said by the Sinhalese chronicle only to have been eleven years old at the time. His military fame speedily grew, and he was soon to become the terror of the Portuguese. Vīdiyē Bandāra, after taking refuge in the hill-country, fled to Mundakondapola in Kurunēgala District, where he repaid his host by taking his life and usurping his principality. Ejected thence by Rājasinha and the Portuguese he fled to Jaffna, where he was murdered in a quarrel, and his treasures fell into the hands of the king of that place. Among these was a relic which the Portuguese were told was Buddha's tooth.

About 1557 Dharmapāla received baptism, taking the name of John, with the result that many of his subjects abandoned him. After besieging Kōttē, Rājasinha continued the war, and in 1561 defeated the Portuguese in the hard contested battle of Mulleriyāwa. Colombo as well as Kōttē were invested in 1563, and, though they were relieved, the capital again was besieged in 1564 with such strictness that the garrison was in a precarious condition by the beginning of the following year. The siege was raised once more, but Rājasinha in reality had the advantage, as the Portuguese abandoned Kōtte and retired on Colombo, taking Dharmapāla with them. Hostilities continued and in 1579-80 Colombo was besieged for one and a half years. About 1580 Rājasinha turned his attention to Kandy and succeeded in annexing that kingdom, expelling the royal family. The deposed king fled to Trincomalee, but shortly afterwards died of smallpox, designating his nephew, later baptized as Dom Philip, as his successor during the minority of his infant daughter Dona Catharina. Vīrasundara, a scion of the Pērādeniya branch of the royal house, had betrayed his own sovereign and joined Rājasinha. But he soon conspired against his new master, who did him to death by treachery ; his son Konappu fled to Colombo. In 1581 Māyādunnē died, poisoned it was alleged by his son, and Rājasinha thus became master of all Ceylon with the exception of Colombo and the north.

The kingdom of Jaffna had not been disturbed by the Portuguese until Christian converts in the Island of Mannar were massacred by the king in 1544. Vengeance was not exacted until 1560, when the Viceroy Dom Constantino de Braganza invaded the peninsula and drove the king into the jungles of the mainland. Tendering his submission, the king took advantage of his return to organize a rising and the Portuguese were compelled to retire. They did not regain their hold on Jaffna until

1591, though Mannar remained in their hands. It was in the expedition of 1560 that the Portuguese obtained

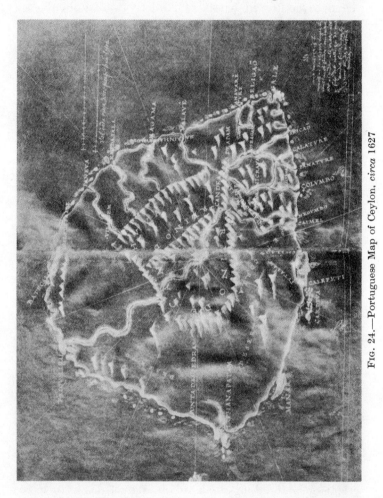

FIG. 24.—Portuguese Map of Ceylon, *circa* 1627

possession of the treasure of Vīdiyē Bandāra and with it of the supposed Tooth Relic. A large sum was offered

for its ransom by the king of Pegu, but was refused, and
the Relic was burnt by the Viceroy at Goa.
Rājasinha I. (A.D. 1581-1593), though a stout warrior,
has a somewhat sinister reputation, due among the Portuguese to his persistent hostility and among the Buddhists
to his rejection of their faith and his adoption of Hinduism.
Having destroyed Kōttē, he aimed at the capture of
Colombo and the total expulsion of the Portuguese. The
fortress was besieged from 1587 to 1588, early in which
year it was relieved. It was at this juncture that the
Portuguese ravaged the coast and destroyed the famous
Vishnu temple at Dondra. In 1590 Rājasinha again was
threatening Colombo. Vīrasundara's son, Konappu Bandāra, known to the Portuguese as Dom John of Austria,
had greatly distinguished himself in the late siege ; he had
no love for Rājasinha, who had murdered his father, and
now offered his services to create a diversion in the Kandyan kingdom. Accordingly he went thither, taking with
him the claimant of the throne of the hill-country and his
son as well as a Portuguese force. Dom Philip was
duly placed upon the throne, and a fort at Gannoruwa
built for his protection against Rājasinha. But the new
king died suddenly, not without suspicion of treachery ;
and Konappu, turning upon the Portuguese at Gannoruwa,
defeated them and proclaimed himself king under the
name of Vimala Dharma Sūrya I. (A.D. 1590-1604). In
1592 Rājasinha attacked his new rival, but was defeated ;
in retiring a bamboo splinter pierced his foot and he died
of blood poisoning early in 1593. As he was only eleven
years old in 1555 he was under fifty at the time of his
death, and the story that he was a centenarian is a myth.
With Rājasinha's demise his kingdom collapsed. His
favourite general Manampēri deserted to Dharmapāla, and
with his help the Portuguese soon annexed the Sītāwaka

dominions and captured the royal princes ; among them
was Nikapitiyē Bandāra, who was removed to Portugal
and died at Coimbra in 1608.

In 1591 the king of Jaffna was unwise enough to attack
Mannar, and in consequence lost his life and throne at the
hands of the Portuguese under Andre Furtado. His
successor, whose rescue from death by Simão Pinhão is
depicted on the mural tablet at the Saman Dēwālē near
Ratnapura, was the creature of Portugal, and from 1593
there were only two powers in the Island, the Kandyans
under Vimala Dharma Sūrya and the Portuguese nomi-
nally fighting for Dharmapāla ; the latter, as we have
seen, had taken Sītāwaka and recovered most of the old
dominions of Kōttē with such ease that in 1594 they
proposed to annex the highland kingdom and place on
the throne Dona Catharina, the daughter of the king
expelled by Rājasinha. Pedro Lopes de Sousa, the first
' Captain General of the Conquest,' succeeded in entering
Kandy, and enthroned the princess. But he alienated
the people by surrounding the young queen with Portuguese. Further, Manampēri was suspected of treason and
slain ; his levies thereupon deserted, and the expedition
ended in disaster in the neighbourhood of Gannoruwa.
The general was killed and Dona Catharina fell into the
hands of Vimala Dharma Sūrya, who perfected his title
by marrying the heiress of Kandy. The ' Apostate of
Candea ' treated the captive Portuguese with great
cruelty, mutilating fifty of them and sending these to
Colombo ' with one eye for each five.'

The Portuguese concentrated at Colombo, awaiting a
general rising of the Sinhalese. This, however, did not
take place, Sītāwaka alone revolting, and Dom Jeronimo
de Azevedo, who was entrusted as Captain General
with orders to retrieve the reputation of Portugal, and

arrived in December of this year 1594, lost no time in setting out in company with the infirm Dharmapāla against the rebels. They were crushed, and stockades erected at Menikkadawara and Ruwanwella, as well as at Galle on the site of the later fortress. In 1595, however, a serious rebellion was raised by Domingos Correa, a Sinhalese subject of Dharmapāla, aided by Vimala Dharma Sūrya, and the old king was compelled to leave Sītāwaka and to fight his way back to Colombo in company with the Portuguese army. For the moment Colombo and Galle alone were left to Dharmapāla. But the tables were turned by the arrival of reinforcements, and Correa was defeated, captured and executed in the middle of 1596. The revolt, however, was continued in a less serious form by Simão Correa, the so-called ' King of Sītāwaka.'

On May 27, 1597, Dharmapāla died. His health had been seriously impaired by poison administered by Māyā-dunnē ; he was childless, and by his Donation, dated August 12, 1580, had bequeathed his dominions and the overlordship of Ceylon to the king of Portugal. Accordingly Philip I. of Portugal and II. of Spain was proclaimed by Dom Jeronimo de Azevedo. The oath of allegiance to the new monarch was taken at Colombo, and thereafter delegates from various divisions of the kingdom were summoned to Malwāna to decide whether they would be governed by the laws of Portugal or by those of Ceylon ; the latter were adopted, and the General agreed to maintain them, insisting however on liberty for Christianity. The theory sometimes put forward that the Sinhalese accepted the king of Portugal on condition that their customs were observed is incorrect.

By January 1599 the fortification of Menikkadawara was complete, and this post now became the chief military centre of the Portuguese, and the seat of the Captain

Major of the army. The war with Kandy continued with
varying fortunes, the difficulties of the Portuguese being
increased by rebellions fomented in different parts of the
country by Vimala Dharma Sūrya. Once the king offered
peace, but the Portuguese who well knew the ' Apostate
of Candea,' did not trust him, and hostilities continued,
waged by either party with incredible ferocity. The
Portuguese ultimately succeeded in reducing the low
country. In 1602 the king attempted to win over Simão
Pinhão, the Portuguese commander-in-chief of the lascorins or native levies. On the instructions of De
Azevedo, Pinhão pretended to enter into the plot with the
object of securing Balanē, the stronghold on the Kadu-
gannāwa range commanding the old road to Kandy ; but
his intentions were revealed to the king by a renegade,
and, though Balanē was stormed in February 1603 the
Portuguese found themselves deserted by their native
troops and were forced to evacuate the place. The
' Great Retreat ' was conducted by the General with skill,
but the position of the Portuguese in a country in full
revolt for a time was precarious : it had improved somewhat by the death of the king in 1604.

In 1602 the Dutchman Joris Spilbergen arrived at
Batticaloa and entered into negotiations with Vimala
Dharma Sūrya. He was the forerunner of the Admiral
Sebald de Weert, who later in the year also put in at the
same port and visited the king. The mission, however,
came to nothing, as Vimala Dharma Sūrya, who was
pressed to go on board the flagship, was suspicious of De
Weert's intentions, and the Admiral, being drunk, insulted
the king and was killed, all the Dutchmen on whom he
could lay his hands also being massacred. This took
place in June 1603. Such was the inauspicious beginning
of the alliance between the Kandyans and the Dutch.

Vimala Dharma Sūrya showed his zeal for the Buddhist religion, which he had again professed on seizing the Kandyan kingdom, by building a two-storied temple for the Tooth Relic. This he had brought from Delgamuwa, close to Kuruwita in Sabaragamuwa, where it is said to have been kept concealed after its removal from Kōttē : its detention there requires further investigation. The king also sent an embassy to Aracan for the purpose of renewing the priestly succession, which once more had failed, and in A.B. 2146 (A.D. 1603/4) held a great Ordination festival at Getambē near Kandy.

Vimala Dharma Sūrya died in 1604, leaving his kingdom to his first cousin Senarat (1604-1635), a priest, who threw off his robes and married his predecessor's widow, Dona Catharina. His accession is dated by Sinhalese authorities in A.B. 2147 (A.D. 1604) and in A.B. 2152 (A.D. 1609/10), the succession having been disputed by Māyādunnē of Uva. The Portuguese naturally took advantage of the civil war to improve their position, and in 1611 advanced to Balanē and burnt Kandy. This campaign was followed by a truce.

On March 8, 1612, the Dutchman Marcellus de Boschouwer arrived at the Sinhalese capital, and on May 11 entered into an agreement with the king, undertaking to secure help from the Netherlands East India Company : his stay in Ceylon, however, was prolonged for three years.

In December 1612 Dom Jeronimo de Azevedo became Viceroy. In eighteen years he had reduced all the districts below Balanē : his most famous exploit was the 'Great Retreat.' His character is stained by the atrocious cruelty with which he carried on the war with Kandy and suppressed the revolts in Portuguese territory. De Queyroz definitely states that no accusation of the kind was made against him during his administration elsewhere, and that he resorted to these excesses in retaliation for those perpetrated by Vimala Dharma Sūrya, to oust whom was his dream. Stern measures doubtless were necessary in dealing with the situation, but nothing can excuse De Azevedo's actions. His methods did not meet with the approval of the authorities in Portugal, and his imprisonment in Lisbon, though on another account, was thought by some to be a retribution for his brutalities in Ceylon.

His successor was Dom Francisco de Meneses. The king, holding that he was no longer bound by the truce now that De Azevedo had departed, broke the peace. The Captain General retaliated by invading the Kandyan territory, but on retiring was attacked at Balanē, whence on being relieved he went to his headquarters at Malwāna. His place was taken in May 1614 by Manuel Mascarenhas Homem, who arrived with minute instructions from the Viceroy for the reform of the army and of the native levies, and for the putting down of oppression and rapine by the soldiers and others. The war was to be prosecuted without mercy, no male over fourteen years of age being spared, and the king was to be cut off from his commerce at Batticaloa, Trincomalee and Jaffna, which last kingdom was to be reduced to the position of a Portuguese dependency. The impotence of Senarat was shown by three expeditions undertaken by the General in 1615 : ˙in January the Portuguese overran Gampola, Maturata and Badulla, returning to Malwāna by way of Sabaragamuwa ; in August, Tumpanē, Hārispattu and Mātalē were plundered ; and a third campaign ensued towards the end of the year. The same policy was continued by Nuno Alvares Pereira, who became Captain General in 1616.

The good fortune of the Portuguese, however, received a severe check by the appearance of a pretender claiming to be the Sītāwaka prince Nikapitiyē Bandāra. The revolt began in the Seven Kōralēs, and with assistance from Kandy soon became general. The Portuguese were in straits, but in 1617 luckily the pretender quarrelled with Senarat, one of whose queens he had asked to wife. Meanwhile one Barreto, a Sinhalese, rebelled in Sabaragamuwa both against the king and against the Portuguese, and secured possession of this province as well as that of Mātara, thus holding the greater part of the south-west of the Island. The self-styled Nikapitiyē Bandara, however, was defeated and fled, and in July the Four and Seven Kōralēs had made their submission. Senarat already had sued for peace, but the removal of the pretender encouraged him, and by the treaty of August 24, 1617, he secured Trincomalee, Batticaloa and Pānama, paying the king of Portugal two elephants yearly. The Portuguese now were free to turn against Barreto. Nikapitiyē, however, reappeared in the Seven Kōralēs, but was not well received and left the scene for good in October. Barreto seems to have been left alone, as when Constantino de Sa de Noronha succeeded in 1618 he found the army a lawless rabble in consequence of the peace.

The new Captain General set about the restoration of discipline, built a stronghold at Sabaragamuwa and laid the foundations of the fortress of S. Cruz at Galle, which was completed in 1625. Māyādunnē, who had fled to India, now returned and, supported by Barreto, came to an open rupture with Senarat ; he was attacked by De Sa and his capital Meddēgama burnt. Jaffna now occupied the General's attention. The king set up by Furtado died in 1615, and the royal power was wielded in the name of his infant son by one Sangili. The regent's attitude towards the Portuguese was equivocal : he had given an asylum to Nikapitiyē Bandāra and was about to be supported by a Malabar fleet. De Sa, therefore, in spite of the danger of dividing his forces, in 1619 dispatched

his Captain Major Philippe de Oliveira to deal with
Jaffna : the kingdom was reduced to subjection, the
native dynasty deposed, and Sangili himself captured and
sent to Goa, where he was tried and executed. Attempts
to recover the country were made in the two following
years by the Naik of Tanjore, who claimed to be the
suzerain, but without success. The fort of Our Lady of
Miracles was built at Jaffna, and the kingdom remained
a Portuguese province until its capture by the Dutch in
1658.

About this time a new European power appeared in
Ceylon. Marcellus de Boschouwer had left the Kandyan
Court in 1615, and after trying to get the Dutch at Batavia
to come to Senarat's assistance, sailed for Holland. Here
he quarrelled with the Company and in 1617 went to
Denmark. In that country an East India Company had
been formed, and King Christian, after concluding a
treaty with the Kandyan plenipotentiary, fitted out a
squadron under the command of Ove Giedde. De Boschouwer died on the voyage. The Danes on their arrival
in Ceylon in 1620 were mortified at finding that the document purporting to be the appointment of the Dutchman
as the Kandyan envoy was a forgery, and that Senarat
refused to confirm the treaty of 1618. A new engagement,
however, was concluded at Bintenna on August 22, 1620,
by which the king ceded to Denmark the territory of
Trincomalee with permission to build a fort. But this
fort was never finished, and the newcomers were expelled
by the Portuguese. About this time Barreto was killed,
and Māyādunnē, who had stirred up the Seven Kōralēs,
once more fled to India.

In 1622 De Sa was replaced for a short time by Jorge
de Albuquerque, who built a fort at Kalutara, but resumed
the government in the following year. During this period

of administration he built forts at Trincomalee (1624), and later at Batticaloa (1628), with the object of controlling the Kandyan trade, and improved the fortifications at Colombo, Galle (1625) and Menikkadawara (1627). He also attempted to reform the civil government, and put a stop to the sale of munitions to and private trade with the Kandyan king on the part of the Portuguese officials. It was in 1626 that on the orders of King Philip he expelled the Moors, the inveterate enemies of the Portuguese ; a large number were settled by the Kandyan Court in the neighbourhood of Batticaloa, where their descendants are still to be found.

De Sa had orders to preserve the peace but to be ready for war should it become necessary to break off relations with Kandy. The building of the stronghold at Batticaloa in 1628 led to hostilities on the part of the king, who found himself encircled by a ring of fortresses on the coast. This he attempted to stop, and encouraged by the death of De Oliveira sent troops to cause a diversion at Jaffna. But De Sa took the opportunity afforded by the division of the enemy forces and invaded the Kandyan territory. In 1629 the Captain General again invaded and succeeded in burning Kandy ; Senarat, or rather his son Rājasinha, claimed to have inflicted a reverse on the Portuguese at Ambatenna, but its date is uncertain. Both sides were exhausted, and the king sued for peace, pending, according to De Queyroz, the maturing of the plot to entrap the Captain General with his army in Uva, and to seize Colombo behind his back, in which Dom Theodosio and three other Sinhalese chiefs in the Portuguese service were engaged. De Sa was ready to agree, but received orders from the Viceroy to reduce Kandy once and for all, and against his better judgment prepared to carry out his instructions. It was about this time that

Rājasinha II., who in a letter to the Dutch in 1636 dates his accession seven years before, was made co-regent with his father. The plot was now ready and Rājasinha's half-brother Kumārasinha made two incursions into Portuguese territory, retiring into Uva. On the entreaties of the conspirators De Sa advanced to punish the prince. Badulla was burnt, but the Portuguese army, deserted by the native levies, fell into a trap and was annihilated at Randeniwela in Lower Uva, the General himself losing his life, on August 24, 1630. The defeat was disastrous to the Portuguese arms : the whole country fell into the king's hands, and Colombo itself was first closely besieged and then blockaded for three months. In 1631 a new plot to kill the new Captain General, Dom Philippe Mascarenhas, and to seize Colombo was discovered. He was succeeded in October of this year by Dom Jorge de Almeida, who arrived with instructions to treat with the king for the recovery of the Portuguese prisoners. He had been in hopes of recovering the Portuguese territories without war in view of the king's known desire for peace, but on the failure of his negotiations advanced in January 1632 and carried the ' Great Stockade ' at Gurubebilē (Hanwella), where one of the slain was an English master-gunner in the Kandyan service. Dom Theodosio, one of the Sinhalese conspirators against De Sa, now quarrelled with the king and made his peace with the Portuguese, and an almost general submission ensued. The king, who was more afraid of Dom Theodosio than of De Almeida, soon sued for peace, and a treaty was signed at Goa on April 15, 1633. By this the rights of the three sons of Dona Catharina were recognized, the king paid an annual tribute of one elephant, and the Portuguese were confirmed in the possession of Batticaloa and recovered their prisoners. But the king, on the execution of Dom

Theodosio by the Portuguese, refused to ratify the treaty, rejecting the stipulation of vassalage.   Diogo de Mello de Castro (1633-1635, 1636-1638), the new Captain General, prepared to fight, but in January 1634, at the very last moment, the king changed his mind and decided to adhere to the Goa treaty.   De Mello's government

FIG. 25.—Portuguese Ceylon Tanga.

was interrupted for a short period by the restoration of De Almeida (1635-1636), whose rule was only signalized by a successful mutiny of the troops.

AUTHORITIES FOR CHAPTER VII

For general history see under Chapter VI. ; also, Ribeiro, *Fatalidade Historica da Ilha de Ceilão*, and João Rodriguez de Sa e Menezes, *Rebelion de Ceylan* (*J.R.A.S., C.B.* xi. No. 41). For the plunder of Kōttē and Sītāwaka see S. Botelho's *Thesouro do Rei de Ceilão*, Lisbon, Academia Real das Sciencias, 1904. For the Saman Dēwālē mural tablet see *J.R.A.S., C.B.* xvi. No. 50, p. 84 ; the episode of the Jaffna prince was only known on the publication of *De Q.* p. 367 (Rev. S. G. Perera, *C.A.* viii. pp. 1 ff.).

For the ' Convention ' of Malwāna, see Ribeiro, book i. chap. 9 ; the better informed De Q. relates the oath of fealty and the proclamation at Colombo, p. 430, and the Convention and its objects on pp. 833, 834. He also gives the text of the petition of 1636, which mentions the Convention on p. 834. For the embassy to Aracan and the restoration of the Upasampadā succession see *Rājavansaya* (Colombo Museum MS.). The Sinhalese dates for the accession of Senarat appear in *Rājavansaya* and the Dambulla Vīhāra tudupata (Lawrie's *Gazetteer*, i. p. 126).

For De Azevedo's cruelties see *De Q.* pp. 400, 401, 488.

For the Danish expedition see the ' Diary of Ove Giedde,' in *A Selection from Danish History, Numismatology, Economics and Language,* Johann Heinrich Schlegel, Copenhagen, 1771. The Ambatenna engagement is mentioned in the *Parangi Hatanē* ; the *Jornada do Reino de Huua* speaks of it as a Portuguese success.

The date of Rājasinha's accession as co-regent is deduced from his letter to the Governor of Pulicat (*J.R.A.S., C.B.* xviii. No. 55, p. 169).

For the later kings of Jaffna see Rev. S. Gnana Prakasar, *The Kings of Jaffna,* Jaffna, 1920.

For De Sa's disastrous expedition into Uva see *Jornada do Reino de Huua,* Codice 51, iv. 32, in the Bibliotheca da Ajuda, Lisbon ; this account is by an eyewitness.

CHAPTER VIII

THE DECLINE OF THE PORTUGUESE POWER
1635-1656

SENARAT had divided his kingdom between his own son Rājasinha, to whom were allotted the ' Five Countries above the mountains,' practically the modern Kandy District, with the title of king, and the other sons of Dona Catharina, Kumārasinha and Vijayapāla, who obtained Uva and Mātalē respectively. Kumārasinha was poisoned by Rājasinha before Senarat's death, which took place in 1635, and the youngest prince became sole king as Rāja-sinha II. (A.D. 1635-1687). The treaty of 1634 was not very strictly observed, and the new sovereign speedily called in the assistance of the Dutch in 1636, offering them a fort at Kottiyār or Batticaloa and guaranteeing the expenses of the fleet. The authorities of the East India Company at Batavia, who already had their eyes on the

Ceylon cinnamon trade, seized the opportunity and instructed their Admiral, Adam Westerwold, who was setting out to blockade Goa, to call at Ceylon on his return voyage. Meanwhile envoys were sent to Rājasinha, at whose court they arrived in 1637. After some negotiations they in company with three Sinhalese went on to join Westerwold off Goa, and were witnesses of an action between the Dutch and Portuguese fleets, in which the latter was worsted in January 4, 1638. The Admiral then decided to send in advance of himself the Vice-Com-

FIG. 26.—Kandyan Silver Fanam and Larin.

mandeur Coster with a small squadron, which arrived at Trincomalee on April 3.

Meanwhile the Captain General Diogo de Mello was indignant at what he termed Rājasinha's treachery in dealing with the Dutch, to prevent which he intrigued with the Prince of Mātalē ; he was further incensed by a private quarrel with the king, and invaded his dominions. Kandy was burnt, but the Portuguese were cut up and the General himself killed at Gannoruwa on March 28, 1638. As usual a widespread revolt ensued, and the king reduced all the Portuguese territory but did not attack the fortresses. Dom Antonio Mascarenhas arrived in May as Captain General (1638-1640), but remained inactive until the end of the year, when on receiving reinforcements he set out to recover the low-country for the Crown of Portugal, in which he succeeded early in 1639.

Coster appeared before Batticaloa on April 8, 1638, and prepared for an attack on the fort. He was joined on May 10 by Westerwold, and a few days later Rājasinha made his appearance with an army. The repeated orders of the king of Portugal issued as early as 1617 for the proper fortification of Trincomalee and Batticaloa had been ignored by the local Government, and as a result the garrison was compelled to surrender on May 18. Westerwold now entered into a treaty with the king. This was signed on the twenty-third and provided for a practical monopoly of the export trade of Ceylon by the Dutch, in return for the assistance given by them to the king, who moreover bound himself to pay all expenses and to hold no communication with the Portuguese. By the third article, which later gave rise to much trouble, all Portuguese forts captured were to be garrisoned by the Dutch, provided that the king did not require them to be demolished. This proviso appeared in the Portuguese copy signed by him ; it was absent, however, from the Dutch.

Shortly afterwards Westerwold left for Batavia, leaving Coster behind at Batticaloa. Trincomalee capitulated on May 2, 1639, the royal forces only appearing after the Dutch had entered the fort. The king then desired that Colombo should be taken. The Council at Batavia, in spite of their unfavourable opinion of Rājasinha's trustworthiness, decided to comply with his wishes, but held it necessary to enter into a more binding agreement, by which all forts taken should be held by the Dutch. The fleet dispatched for the purpose under the command of Philip Lucasz, with Coster as Vice-Admiral, arrived at Trincomalee in December, only to find that the garrison had been deliberately starved by Rājasinha. Early in January 1640 the fleet sailed for Colombo, but seeing that it was hopeless to carry the place owing to the failure of Rājasinha to appear landed the troops near Negombo, where they were joined later on by the Sinhalese. Negombo was taken on February 4, and was garrisoned by the Dutch, at which Rājasinha took umbrage and retired. Coster, however, succeeded in inducing the king to enter into a new agreement ; in this it was settled that when the Portuguese had been completely expelled from Ceylon the Dutch should retain only one fort, but that they should hold Negombo and the other forts until all the expenses of the war had been paid, and that Colombo, when captured, should be demolished unless the king decided that it should be kept as a fortress, in which case it was to be garrisoned by the Dutch. The king's indebtedness in this year amounted to 310,790 pieces-of-eight.

The fleet now sailed southwards, and Galle was stormed on March 13, the Sinhalese again arriving too late to take part in the fighting. The king was still dissatisfied with the Dutch, and Coster followed him to Kandy in the hope of bringing about a better understanding. Nothing came of the negotiations, and Coster leaving in disgust was murdered on his way back to Batticaloa by the Sinhalese. The king, though he expressed his regret, clearly was better pleased to see the Dutch and Portuguese fight each other than to give the former loyal assistance and ensure the fall of Colombo, which was then feasible. The position of the Dutch in the Island between the Sinhalese and the Portuguese was not happy.

The Captain General Dom Philippe Mascarenhas (1640-1645) arrived with reinforcements and retook Negombo on November 9, 1640. The Portuguese, though not strong enough to besiege Galle, encamped in the neighbouring country and towards the end of the year reduced to obedience the Four and Seven Kōralēs, while Rājasinha held Sabaragamuwa. Things went still better in their favour owing to the civil war, which broke out in 1641 in the Kandyan territory between the king and Vijayapāla. The latter, however, was compelled to fly to Colombo, but, instead of being kept as a weapon against Rājasinha, was sent to Goa in compliance with an old order of the king of Portugal that heathen princes were not to be restored unless converted to the Christian faith ; he died in exile in 1654. His removal to Goa may have been due to his intrigues with the Dutch in 1643.

From June 1642 Galle was closely blockaded by land, Rājasinha giving his allies no assistance, until February 1643 when news was brought of the treaty of peace lasting ten years entered into between the Dutch and John IV., the first of the restored native dynasty of Portugal, which had thrown off the Spanish yoke in December 1640. But the Dutch under Jan Thyszoon (1640-1646) claimed the country round Galle as the appurtenance of the fortress, though they were not in possession. The matter was referred to Goa, and the Viceroy refusing to comply with the Dutch demands the war continued. Towards the end of the year the Dutch were reinforced ; in January 1644 they retook Negombo and made an attempt on Colombo, but failed. Later on in the year orders were received from Portugal to give up all territories belonging exclusively to the forts held by the Dutch at the time of their publication at Goa ; a truce to last for eight years was signed on November 10, 1644, and the agreement as to the details at Colombo on January 10 following. The Portuguese thus lost far more than they would have had hostilities ended in 1643, for the Dutch now obtained part of the Seven Kōralēs in the neighbourhood of Negombo as well as the whole of the Mātara disāvany or province south of the Bentota River. The boundary between the present Western and Southern Provinces dates from this treaty. Rājasinha, from whom the Company had suffered more than from the avowed enemy, was most indignant at the partition of what he considered as his dominions between the two European powers, the more so as they had concluded on March 9, 1645, a treaty for mutual protection against the highlanders. The Dutch endeavoured to pacify him, but he demanded the withdrawal of their troops from the Seven Kōralēs to Negombo. In May Thyszoon declared war, goaded to this step by Rājasinha's depredations, but did not enjoy much success. His action was disapproved of at Batavia, and he was superseded as Governor in 1646 by Joan Maatzuyker (1646-1650). Van der Stel was dispatched in May to withdraw the troops to Negombo, but unluckily coming into collision with the royal forces, who had advanced so far with the connivance of the Portuguese, imprudently provoked an encounter, in which he and almost all their men lost their lives. The Dutch garrison in the Seven Kōralēs surrendered and were taken prisoners to Kandy. The king now demanded the destruction of Negombo, regardless of Coster's treaty and of his own desire expressed the previous year that the place should be held by the Dutch. Maatzuyker took a firm attitude and openly enquired whether Rājasinha wished peace or war : the former he declared to be impossible unless the prisoners were restored. In 1647 an ambassador was sent to the Court but without result ; the Portuguese were negotiating with Rājasinha, who entered into an alliance with them in spite of Maatzuyker's threat that if the Dutch went to war with the Portuguese they would hold the fortresses taken in the name of the States General and not in that of the king. In 1649, however, the king, who in order to prevent the

FIG. 27.—Bird's Eye View of Jaffna, *circa* 1656.

collection of cinnamon by the Dutch had depopulated the
Pitigal Kōralē, had veered round once more, released the
ambassador sent two years before, and negotiated a new

treaty, which differed little from that of 1638 save that the Company no longer was to have the monopoly of cinnamon. In this instrument the treaty with Westerwold is rehearsed, with the missing words of the third article duly inserted in the Dutch. In 1650 Maatzuyker was succeeded by Van Kittensteyn (1650-1653). The Dutch felt no reliance in Rājasinha's good faith, and their position was made more difficult by the king's claim to appoint the Disāwas or provincial governors in the territory held by them. As early as 1650 Rājasinha alleged a breach of the new treaty, and the relations between the two allies continued strained until 1652, when hostilities were recommenced with the Portuguese.

The Captain General, Manoel Mascarenhas Homem, who had succeeded Philippe Mascarenhas in 1645, wished to concentrate his forces at Colombo and abandoned Kalutara, which the Dutch at once occupied. The army was suspicious that he intended betraying them to the Dutch, and mutinied at Menikkadawara ; it then advanced on Colombo, pursued by the king's forces, and under Gaspar Figueira deposed the Captain General and kept him in custody. Figueira, who held the real power and was a man of energy, attacked the Dutch towards Negombo, on January 8, 1653, defeated them at Anguruwātota in Kalutara District, and then turned on the king in the Four Kōralēs, stationing his forces at Arandara. On May 10 Francisco de Mello de Castro (1653-1655) arrived to succeed Homem, whom he released ; he brought a pardon for the mutineers which they refused to accept, holding that they had saved the Portuguese possessions in the Island. The war continued, generally in favour of the Portuguese, Kalutara falling into their hands after a blockade lasting from July 1653 to March 1654. But the Dutch were only awaiting reinforcements, which at length arrived under Gerard Hulft, Director General of the land and sea forces, in September 1655. The days of the Portuguese were numbered. On October 14 Kalutara surrendered. The Dutch at once closed on Colombo, and after a desperate resistance, in which the garrison was reduced to famine, Antonio de Sousa Coutinho (1655-1656), was obliged to capitulate on May 12, 1656, after a siege lasting six months and twenty-seven days, to the Governor Van der Meyden (1653-1662), Hulft having been killed on April 10. Rājasinha had only appeared early in 1656. The Dutch clearly were anxious not to have the shifty king too near during the operations ; his presence with his army actually contributed little or nothing to the issue of the siege. The defence of Colombo against overwhelming odds was the most gallant feat of the Portuguese in Ceylon.

THE PORTUGUESE ADMINISTRATION, 1597-1656

The Portuguese Government of Ceylon was subject to the Viceroy at Goa. At its head was the Captain General, with his residence at Malwāna ; he was spoken of by the natives as the king of Malwāna, with the title of Highness. He was assisted by a Vedor da Fazenda, in charge of the revenue, and by an Ouvidor or judge. The ' City of St. Lawrence ' or Colombo was administered by a Chamber or municipal body.

The country was divided into four disāvanies or provinces, each under a Disāwa or governor, who possessed much greater powers than under the native kings. These provinces were Mātara, including the whole of the present Southern Province and the Kolonna Kōralē, the Kalutara District and the Salpiti Kōralē ; the Four Kōralēs, comprising the northern part of the Kēgalla District with the Siyanē and Hāpitigam Kōralēs ; the Seven Kōralēs, or the Alutkūru Kōralē, the whole of the North Western Province, and in theory much of the North Central ; and Sabaragamuwa, that is the Three Kōralēs and Bulatgama of Kēgalla District, the Hēwāgam Kōralē, and the Ratnapura District less Kolonna Kōralē. The disāvanies thus radiated from Kōttē. A Disāwa of Negombo appears in 1640. Each Kōralē or division of a disāvany was under an Adigar, the later Kōralē Vidānē or Kōrāla, each pattu or subdivision was under an Atukōrāla, while in each village were mayorals or kāriyakarannō, supervised by a Vidānē in the case of the royal villages and those granted during pleasure or for a life or term of lives to Portuguese and others. All or almost all the land was held by service tenure, often military in character ; there was little revenue in cash. Royal monopolies were :

Cinnamon, first collected by the Salāgama people under Rājasinha I. They were organized under the Captain of the Mahabadda ;

Areca and pepper, which the owners were compelled to sell to the Government at a fixed price ;

Precious stones, in Sabaragamuwa ;

Elephants, which were sold in India ; and, lastly, the Pearl Fishery.

The Disāwas possessed civil, including judicial, as well as military jurisdiction over the natives of the country. Further, a tribunal of the Captain General's 'banacas' (banneka or basnāyaka) or secretaries assisted him in the disposal of such cases as came before him. Every year what may be called assizes were held in the country, for the primary purpose of collecting the marāla or death duty, one maralleiro for each disāvany appointed by the Bandigērāla, originally perhaps a treasury officer, visiting his province, assisted by two interpreters of the laws, a

sheriff and a secretary. Under the native kings, if there
were no male heir to a service holding, the whole escheated
to the Crown ; otherwise it was heritable on payment of
one-third of the movables of the deceased. This last
share was that taken
by the Portuguese in
the former case also,
Christians being ex-
empted from this im-
post.   The   assizes
dealt not only with
the estates of deceased
persons, but also with
civil   and   criminal
matters, such as debt,
theft, and murder. If
the   murderer   was
arrested within sixty
days the General or
Disāwa   condemned
him to death offhand,
but had no power to
do so after the elapse
of that period, when
the   criminal   could
confess at the assizes
and compound.   No
such privilege, how-

FIG. 28.—Bird's Eye View of Colombo,
circa 1656.

ever, existed where a low caste man had killed one of high
caste.   Questions of caste such as irregular marriages
also came before the assizes, and the ordeals of oil, red-
hot iron, and the like were in use. A sanctuary existed
at Galle for all crimes save treason, false coining, and the
murder of a sheriff or judge. The system of criminal

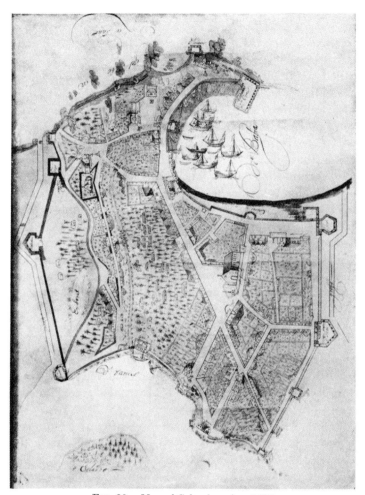

FIG. 29.—Map of Colombo, *circa* 1656.

jurisprudence should be compared with that prevailing in the tenth century.

In military matters the Captain Major of the Field was

the chief Portuguese officer under the Captain General ; his headquarters were at Menikkadawara. The principal fortresses were Colombo, Galle and Jaffna. The Portuguese troops were either casados or married men, only called upon in an emergency, and the soldados, whose discipline practically disappeared in time of peace, and who then were little better than brigands. This is not surprising, as at one time service in Ceylon was an alternative to prison. The native levies or Lascarins were under the Disāwa, and under the supreme command of the Vikramasinha, the Senevirad of earlier times. He alone under the kings of Kōttē with the exception of the royal family was allowed the use of a palanquin. The Lascarins, who served for fifteen days at a time, were armed with swords, bows and arrows, spears or muskets. The artillery attached to these levies consisted of gingals ; these were light portable pieces of ordnance, somewhat after the fashion of an enormous pistol supported in front by two legs and throwing a ball of some four to twelve ounces in weight, and were fired by the gunner in a sitting posture. The Portuguese do not seem to have employed elephants in warfare, though these beasts were used by Rājasinha I. in besieging Colombo, and, with swords and knives fastened to their trunks, were wont to lead the van of the Sinhalese army.

Jaffna was under a separate administration, subject however to the Captain General, the chief officers being the Captain Major of the Kingdom, the Factor and the Ouvidor. Mannar was under a Captain, who lost much of his importance when Jaffna was conquered.

In ecclesiastical affairs the Island formed part of the diocese of Cochin, whose Bishop governed through a Vicar-General. The first missionaries were Franciscans, but shortly after 1600 the Jesuits, the Dominicans, and the

Augustinians came into the field in addition to the secular clergy. The Franciscans had been given the temple villages by Dharmapāla in 1591, but were deprived of them by the civil authorities, whose indifference and opposition to the enterprise of the clergy was a matter of grievance. In the three Franciscan ' Colleges,' attached to the monasteries, there were taught religion, good manners (*mores*), reading, writing and arithmetic, singing, and Latin. There were also parish schools ; of these in Jaffna the Franciscans had twenty-five and the Jesuits twelve. The latter Order also had colleges in Jaffna and Colombo for higher education. All education was free.

So much has been published as to the iniquities of the Portuguese that little remains to be said. Corruption and peculation prevailed in all departments of the administration. The Sinhalese had chosen to abide by their own laws at the meeting at Malwāna in 1597. These were never codified, and much of the tyranny and violence suffered by the people was due to the Portuguese under the influence of avarice carrying out the native system of government to its logical conclusion, regardless of the restraining influence of custom. For example, areca undoubtedly was a monopoly of the last Kandyan kings, and we have seen in the tenth century that fruit trees could be cut down in the villages : both these rights were carried to excess by the new lords to the total impoverishment of the people. Under the old government the chiefs had a wholesome fear of the king, who, if a strong ruler, suffered no tyrant but himself; under the Portuguese every lord of a village, nay, every petty headman, assumed powers which would not have been tolerated before. It must be remembered that the worst enemies of the villager often were his own fellow-countrymen ; the Vidānēs were as bad as any Portuguese village lord, and the Lascarins

C.C.   I

in 1636 actually prayed for Portuguese instead of Sinhalese Mudaliyārs and Ārachchis, a prayer curiously reminiscent of a similar request by the people at Kandy in 1815.

In the army the total lack of discipline in time of peace and the peculation of their pay by their superiors turned soldiers into armed highway robbers. The constant wars added to the harassing of the people by perpetual services led to the depopulation of much of the country, and at the end of the Portuguese rule the Disāvany of Mātara could only supply 1500 Lascarins against 4000 under De Azevedo. The popular discontent was not allayed by the destruction of the temples, an unwise proceeding in the unsettled state of the country, though it is only fair to say that in certain cases, such as that of the Munnēssaram pagoda, the temples were destroyed in retaliation for the burning of churches.

But there is another side to the picture. We must put a De Sa against a De Azevedo. The clergy, though they were keen on the service of His Majesty as well as on the service of God, usually were on the side of the people against their oppressors. The fact that their converts, as in Japan, retained the Christian religion in spite of lack of clergy and active persecution by the Dutch, speaks much in their favour, and such a result cannot have come from a nation wholly bad. In another sphere to the Portuguese is due the introduction of chillies, tobacco, and a number of foreign fruit trees. And one cannot withhold admiration for the pluck and endurance with which a few hundred men, fighting in a tropical climate, succeeded in reducing so large a territory. It is interesting to speculate what the history of Ceylon would have been had the Portuguese not ventured to India. There seems to be little doubt that the kingdom of Vijayanagar would have collapsed earlier than it did, and that the south of India and with it

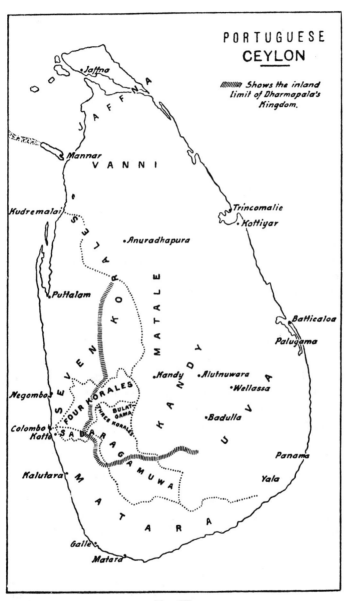

MAP VI.

possibly Ceylon would have fallen under Muhammadan rule.

We hear much of ' Sinhalese perfidy ' in the Portuguese writers. The complaint, however, does not seem to come into prominence until the reduction of the low-country by the Portuguese after the death of Rājasinha I., when the inhabitants, whose sympathies naturally lay with the native dynasty, were harried by the Kandyans if they remained faithful to Portugal, and by the Portuguese if they sided with Kandy. The charge is far more true in the case of the Kandyan Government, on whose word no reliance was to be placed ; even here it may be held that treachery was the refuge of the weaker power. But this characteristic was evident in the Kandyan dealings with the Dutch, who put up with much for the sake of peace, and is shown in its worst form in the massacre of the British troops in 1803.

According to De Queyroz the kingdom of Kandy comprised the principalities of Uva, Mātalē, Gampola, Batticaloa, Pānama, Kottiyār, and at one time Trincomalee, of which the last four were held by Vanniyars ; the Disāvanīes of Hārispattu, Pansiyapattu or Dumbara, Udunuwara and Yatinuwara, all in the neighbourhood of the capital ; and the territories of Bintenna, Wellassa, and Maturata, administered by Vidānēs.

AUTHORITIES FOR CHAPTER VIII

For general history see *Raj.*, *De Q.*, and Rājasinha's letters published in *J.R.A.S.*, *C.B.* xviii. No. 55 ; also Baldaeus, *Beschryving van het Machtige Eyland Ceylon*; ' Beknopte Historie ' (*J.R.A.S.*, *C.B.* xi. No. 38) ; *De Opkomst van het Nederlandsch Gezag over Ceilon*, W. van Geer, Leiden, 1895.

The date of Senarat's death is given in various Sinhalese verses ; different months are given, but all agree as to the

Saka year 1557. The *Jornada do Reino de Huua* states that he was fifty-eight years old at his demise in 1635. According to this work Senarat ' absolutely was the best captain, the best king, and the best man whom the Chingalas knew ' ; he was learned, liberal and kind to the poor, and most valiant. For Vijayapāla's letter to the Governor of Pulicat received on January 22, 1643, see *Dag Register*, 1643, 1644 (Department van Kolonien). The treaty of March 9, 1645, was for mutual protection against the highlanders, who invaded and devastated the cinnamon lands, chasing the inhabitants out of their villages ; all dealings with the king of Kandy were forbidden (*Opkomst*).

For the city of St. Lawrence see the Donation of Dharma-pāla (*Orientalist*, iii. p. 196). The details as to the provinces of Mātara, the Seven and Four Kōralēs, and Sabaragamuwa are given in *De Q.* pp. 25-36 ; he also gives much information as to the kingdom of Kandy and the various principalities, pp. 45-56. The Disāwa of Negombo is mentioned by *De Q.* p. 705. The administrative system is dealt with by *Ribeiro* and by *De Q.* book vi., and considerable light is thrown on it by the petition of 1636 (*De Q.* pp. 834 ff.). The Kandyan monopoly of areca is described in *Correspondence of the Board of Commissioners*, vol. 521, June 9 and July 24, 1816, January 7 and 8, 1821. In connection with the possibility of Muham-madan rule in Ceylon see *Documentos Remettidos*, i. 57.

CHAPTER IX

THE DUTCH OCCUPATION, 1656-1796

THE terms of the capitulation of Colombo led immediately to a breach between Rājasinha and the Dutch. The king contended that Hulft had promised that Colombo should be delivered to him to be demolished. The Dutch on the other hand had no intention of giving him so important a place, the more so as their expenses in the campaign had not been paid, and alleged that Hulft had understood that the king wished the existing walls to be pulled down and a smaller part of the city fortified, as was actually carried out later.   Rājasinha by this time was for the moment master of Ceylon, with the exception of the north and of the fortresses with some villages on the coast, and proceeded to starve out the Dutch, plundering and well-nigh depopulating the low country.   Collisions occurred, and at last in November, 1656, the Dutch, unable to tolerate longer the state of affairs, drove the king from the vicinity of Colombo.   The low country had been so denuded of its inhabitants that the Company some years later resolved that the lands between Hanwella, Angaruwātota and the coast should be peopled and cultivated by Tanjore slaves and citizens of Colombo.

The year 1657 was spent in the blockade of Goa, and it was only in 1658 that Tuticorin and Mannar fell into the hands of the Dutch.   These captures were completed by the surrender of Jaffna on June 24, 1658, after a siege of three months, and by the consequent total expulsion of the Portuguese from the Island.   The conquest of Jaffna was marked by unnecessary brutality on the part of the Dutch in the treatment of their prisoners.

Van der Meyden was succeeded by Rykloff van Goens the Elder, who governed except for brief intervals from 1660 to 1675.   Relations with the Court of Kandy continued strained, but in 1664 a rebellion broke out against Rājasinha, who fled to Hanguranketa and wrote for help to the Dutch.   Their assistance took the form of annexing fifteen districts in 1665, by which the Company's frontier became practically conterminous with that held by the Portuguese in the Four Kōralēs and Sabaragamuwa, the Seven Kōralēs being left to the Sinhalese : Trincomalee and Batticaloa also were occupied at the same time, Kalpitiya in 1667, and Kottiyār in 1668.   Desultory hostilities on the part of Rājasinha continued, and the Dutch, unable to get satisfaction from the king, closed the ports of Kottiyār, Batticaloa and Kalpitiya, thus stopping the Kandyan trade. In 1671 the king again was in trouble with his own subjects.

About this time the French entered into negotiations with Rājasinha and occupied Trincomalee. They were expelled in 1672 by the Dutch, and their ambassador, who had offended the king, was kept a prisoner in the interior until his death. Peace continued until 1675, when a general insurrection took place, and at the same time an invasion by the Kandyans in force. In this year the Governor was succeeded by his son Rykloff van Goens the Younger (1675-1679), and in 1677 the Batavian authorities ordered the restoration to Rājasinha of the districts occupied twelve years previously. The king, however, made no effort to take them over, and intermittent hostilities continued until the government was assumed by Laurens Pyl (1679-1692), who made a good impression on the Court. But Rājasinha was still angry over the closing of the ports, and in 1684 surprised and secured a considerable amount of territory as well as the invaluable salt pans at Hambantota, all however included in the districts ordered to be returned to him. The efforts of the Company to obtain a permanent peace were still fruitless when the old king died on November 25, 1687.

Rājasinha is well known to us from his correspondence with the Dutch edited by the late Mr. Donald Ferguson, and from the account of the Kandyan kingdom written by the Englishman Robert Knox, detained there with his fellows as a captive from 1659 to 1679. He was a strong ruler and united his dominions, rectifying the disastrous division made by his father by poisoning one half-brother and driving out the other. Despotic and tyrannical, suspicious yet farseeing, he kept his chiefs as hostages at Court, and had no remorse in ravaging and depopulating his subjects' lands when it seemed to his political advantage. He was a master in craft and double dealing, but met his equal in diplomacy in the Dutch, who found it impossible to act otherwise with so shifty an ally. He was acquainted with Portuguese, and probably had a somewhat wider outlook than his successors, who firmly believed that they were the greatest sovereigns on earth and their little kingdom the centre of the world. He had no conception of the law of nations, detaining and even imprisoning ambassadors, apparently regarding such luckless Europeans as fell into his hands as curiosities, much in the same way as the lion and other animals sent him by the Dutch. In military matters he was in no wise the equal of his namesake of Sītāwaka, whom he wished to emulate ; his troops, excellent at guerilla warfare, were unfitted for fighting in the open or for siege work, and their presence at Colombo rather hindered the Dutch than otherwise. The Sinhalese proverb, ' I gave pepper and got ginger,' illustrative of a bad bargain, was applied to his ousting the Portuguese by means of ' the faithful Hollanders,' and his invitation of a strong power only resulted in the isolation of his kingdom and its removal from all progressive influences.

The new king, Rājasinha's son, Vimala Dharma Sūrya II. (1687-1707), demanded in return for peace the freedom of the ports and the cession of the districts taken in 1665 ; these actually were given up in 1688, the Company's frontier thus becoming the existing inland boundaries of the Western and Southern Provinces. The position of the Dutch as protectors of the sea-coast for the king was anomalous, Rājasinha by 1658 having gone so far as to deny any contract, and they found it difficult to control the people of the districts held by them ; moreover, as the cinnamon was largely gathered in the king's territory they were always under obligation to the Court. It was about this time that notice seems to have been taken of the Donation of Dharmapāla, and the Company decided to base its claim to the Maritime Provinces as against Europeans on conquest rather than on treaty and hypothec pending the payment of expenses. The Dutch suggested terms to the Court, one article providing that their old territories and ports should be ceded to the Company in annulment of the king's indebtedness, but their proposals were refused. In spite of this the relations between the two parties remained more or less harmonious during the remainder of Pyl's government and during that of Van Rhee (1692-1697).

In 1701 under Gerrit de Heere (1697-1702) the Kandyans closed the frontiers with the object of stimulating their trade with Puttalam and Kottiyār, the only ports left to them. This step was so successful that Puttalam became the chief place for the areca-nut trade, which thus was lost to the Company, and the frontiers were reopened in 1703. The policy of the Company was to bring pressure to bear upon the king through trade ; in 1703 instructions were sent to the Company's officials in Coromandel, Malabar and the Madura Coast to issue no passports except to Colombo, Galle and Jaffna, and in November 1707 the ports were definitely closed. This step led to considerable friction with the Court, which periodically retaliated by stopping the Dutch trade with the interior. Governor Simons (1702-1706) is responsible for the compilation of the Tēsavalamai or Customary Laws of Jaffna.

Meanwhile in the interior the state of the Buddhist

priesthood called for urgent reform ; the temple lands had become hereditary, and in A.B. 2240 (A.D. 1697/8) the king sent an embassy to Aracan for the purpose of obtaining priests. He also built a three-storied temple for the Tooth Relic in Kandy. His death occurred on June 4, 1707, when he was succeeded by his son, Narēndra Sinha (1707-1739), the last of the Sinhalese dynasty. In his reign the Kandy Maha Dēwālē was founded in 1731.

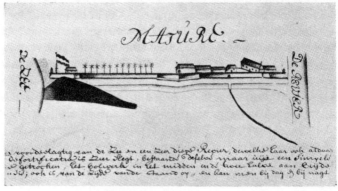

FIG. 30.—Mātara, 1717.

In the time of Governor Rumpf (1716-1723) the Moors of the Coast made an attempt to create a port further to the north of Puttalam, egress from which was blocked by Kalpitiya held by the Dutch ; the plan, however, was frustrated. In 1723 the cinnamon peelers rose in a body against their headmen, but were subdued and in punishment deprived of many privileges. Governor Vuyst (1726-1729) is notorious for his tyrannical rule. He resorted to torture and to inhuman punishments, and general terror prevailed. News, however, reached Batavia, and he was arrested, tried, and executed. Under Pielat (1732-1734), who was sent to investigate grievances, a rebellion occurred, and under Van Domburg (1734-1736) many districts as well as the cinnamon peelers broke into open revolt. The grievances of the people in general were many. Fines were imposed for failure of their children to attend school ; the cultivation of chenas or low jungle periodically cleared and sown was wrongfully monopolized by the headmen, besides being hindered in the interests of cinnamon ; the Company's share in gardens planted ' with consent,' which share was sold at the appraised value to the planter, was raised from one-third to one-half ; and, last of all, exception was taken to the Watubadda, a tax on certain gardens. The cinnamon peelers complained of unjust treatment by their headmen and of heavy taxation. The abolition of the Watubadda as well as of the extra burdens which had been imposed on the peelers, together with permission to clear chenas on direct application to and permit from the Disāwa came too late, and the revolt spread, fostered by the Court. At last the Kandyans joined in openly, annexing the Siyanē, Hāpitigam, and Alutkūru Kōralēs, and formal war was declared in 1736. On the arrival of Van Imhoff (1736-1739) the Court found that it had to do with a strong man and the country grew quieter, but the trouble continued and internal peace was not restored until the end of 1737. The new Governor saw that the cause of the disquiet was the closing of the ports in 1707 and determined to reestablish friendly relations.

The king died on May 13, 1739, and was succeeded by his queen's brother, of the Nāyakkar dynasty of Madura, who came to the throne under the name of Srī Vijaya Rājasinha (1739-1747). The hostility of the Court, and especially of the Dravidian element, continued. In 1740, in spite of the granting of the king's request for a yacht to carry emissaries to Siam, Pegu, Tennasserim and other places for the purpose of obtaining orthodox Buddhist priests, its obstruction was such that no cinnamon was shipped home that year, an attitude perhaps encouraged by the shipwreck of the embassy. Next year there took place several incursions into Dutch territory, the Kandyans going so far as to stop the erection of a church and school, the first symptom of the anti-Christian prejudices of the new dynasty which soon developed into open persecution in the Kandyan country. To all these provocations the Company tamely submitted on the explicit orders from Batavia to avoid a breach with the Court ; but the greater the patience evinced by the Dutch the more outrageous became the Kandyans. A new embassy seems to have been dispatched to Siam at the end of 1741, and in 1742 the Company was required to forward letters by its own servants to Aracan and Siam and to bring back replies. The demand was partially complied with ; yet in 1743 a fresh provocation was offered, the Court annexing nine villages in the Siyanē Kōralē. Protests had a slight effect, but in 1745 the Kandyans again invaded the Dutch territory and had the assurance to ask for a ship to convey an embassy to Pegu. The Dutch at last determined not to yield further and refused the request, with the result that a new aggression took place, the Court claiming seven more villages in the Siyanē Kōralē. These tactics meeting with no success, and depredations having been discontinued, a new request for a ship was granted by Governor Van Gollenesse (1743-1751), who built Wolvendaal Church. The embassy left for Siam in 1746 and succeeded in obtaining priests ; they were about to sail for Ceylon when news was received of the king's death on August 11, 1747, New Style.

The late king was succeeded by his brother-in-law Kīrti Srī (1747-1782). He was a zealous Buddhist, and in

1750 dispatched an embassy to Siam in confirmation of his predecessor's action. The priests arrived in Ceylon in 1753, and re-established the succession, which has not since been lost ; the ' Siamese sect,' thus founded, is in possession of the greater part of the old temples and of their temporalities. Weliwita Saranankara, who had played a leading part in the Buddhist revival since the time of Narēndra Sinha, was made Sangharāja or head of the order ; he died in 1778. This revival was accompanied by persecution. The Catholics, harried and proscribed by the Dutch, had found a refuge in the Kandyan country, where they had been protected or at least tolerated by the Sinhalese kings, and Christianity had received a marked impetus from the labours of the Venerable Father José Vaz, a Brahman from the neighbourhood of Goa, who arrived in the Island in 1687 and died in 1711. But a new spirit characterized the kings of the Madura dynasty, and in 1743 Srī Vijaya Rājasinha destroyed the churches and initiated a persecution, which was continued under Kīrti Srī. It ceased only because the king considered that certain calamities which fell upon the country were due to his action. Kīrti Srī built the existing inner temple of the Tooth Relic, and caused the *Mahāvansa* chronicle to be continued from the time of Parākrama Bāhu IV. down to his own reign.

The Court was still inclined to be quarrelsome, and in 1753 put forward a demand for participation in the elephant trade. The request was repeated more than once, but was always refused on the ground that the old privileges enjoyed by the Company should be maintained.

In 1760 a violent and desperate insurrection broke out throughout the Sinhalese provinces of the Company, the causes as before being largely agrarian, and the discontent being fanned by the Kandyan Court. The people were aggrieved by the methods employed by the renters in collecting the Government dues from the paddy fields, but the chief cause of the revolt was the policy adopted by Governor Schreuder (1757-1762) in resuming for the Company planted lands in the cinnamon-growing areas. For some time past felling of jungle and planting of coconut gardens had become common, and the Government, whose monopoly was affected, resolved in 1758 to expropriate the possessors. Compensation in land elsewhere was to be given to those who held the lots now required in virtue of grants from the Governor or who had paid for such as had been planted without the Company's consent ; but persons who had not paid for lands planted whether with or without consent were to get nothing. Expropriation was not to take place immediately ; after the expiry of four years, by which time the plantations on the newly given lands were expected to be in bearing, the old lots were to be resumed and such trees cut down as were found to be necessary. The cinnamon peelers, as usual, took the opportunity to cause trouble. The Dutch enjoyed a brief respite owing to a conspiracy against the king's life ; the plot was unsuccessful, and in 1761 the Kandyans invaded the low country and had little difficulty in taking Mātara and Hanwella forts, at the same time occupying all the frontier districts. The Dutch retaliated by entering Kandyan territory, but were forced to retire. But the king felt the need of help, and his negotiations with the English East India Company at Madras led to Pybus' fruitless mission in 1762. Later in this year Van Eck (1762-1765) arrived as Governor and at once infused energy into the Dutch. To him is due the Star Fort at Mātara. Chilaw and Puttalam were captured, and in 1763 an expedition was sent into the interior ; it was,

however, unsuccessful owing to the guerilla tactics of the
Kandyans.   But early in 1765 a new attack was made on
the king's country, one army under Van Eck in person
advancing from Colombo through the Seven Kōralēs and
the Galagedara pass, and another marching from Puttalam.
Katugastota was reached on February 16.   The king now
was prepared to make very considerable concessions, and
offered the Company Sabaragamuwa, the Three, Four and
Seven Kōralēs, and the sovereignty of the coasts of the
whole Island.   Van Eck, however, was persuaded, it is said
by Van Angelbeek, afterwards the last Dutch Governor,
to insist on the king taking his crown as the vassal of the
Company.   This Kīrti Srī refused to do and abandoned
the capital, which the Dutch occupied in February 19.
Their energies were wasted in attacks on Hanguranketa
and Kundasālē, and in guerilla warfare.   Van Eck left
Kandy on March 4, and reaching Colombo six days later
died on April 1.   The garrison which had been left behind
in Kandy was poorly provided ; it fell a prey to sickness
and was beleaguered by the exasperated Kandyans, but
fought its way out without loss.   In August Falck
arrived as Van Eck's successor and began negotiations
with the Court.   The Kandyans, who had been unable
to sow their fields, were on the verge of starvation, and the
new Governor brought further pressure to bear on them
by ravaging the Three, Four, and Seven Kōralēs, and by
expeditions into Bintenna and Mātalē.   A little diplomacy
on the part of Falck won the day, and peace was finally
attained by the treaty of February 14, 1766, by which
the king relinquished to the Company the full sovereignty
not only of the territories already held by it but of the
remaining districts bordering on the coast.   The Kandyans
were now completely cut off from the outer world, and
the king in 1772 began a new series of demands for a share

Fig. 31.—Reception of Kandyan Embassy by Governor Falck, 1772.

in the pearl fishery, adding in 1776 another for the restoration of a part of the coast.

The war between Great Britain and the revolted American colonies ultimately involved Holland, and resulted in the fall of Negapatam in 1781. It was at this period that the Company's mint at Tuticorin was transferred to Colombo. Early in January 1782 Trincomalee was captured by the British Admiral Sir Edward Hughes, and Boyd sent as ambassador to Kandy. But Kīrti Srī had died on January 2 of the injuries caused two months before by a fall from his horse, and his brother Rājādhirājasinha (1782-1798) refused to treat with the envoy on the ground that he was not authorized by King George III. Admiral Hughes, who had left a garrison at Trincomalee, fought an indecisive action with the French under Suffren at sea on February 17, and again off Trincomalee on April 12. Another battle was fought on July 4, after which both fleets refitted. On August .25 Suffren reappeared before Trincomalee, and the fort surrendered shortly afterwards, only a few days before the coming of Hughes. Trincomalee was restored to the Company by the French at the Peace of Paris in 1784.

On February 5, 1785, Falck died and was succeeded by Van de Graaff. The new Governor's relations with Kandy were strained. In 1791 the king sent his Disāwas to mobilize the local levies in the border districts ; the Dutch therefore reinforced their frontier garrisons. Their request for an explanation of the unusual activity was met by a demand for the restoration of the coast ; this was refused and the king was requested to withdraw his troops, whereupon the Dutch withdrew theirs. Shortly afterwards the Government, on information supplied by the Adigar Pilama Talauwē, soon to become so well known to the British, intercepted a letter from the king to the French

c.c.   K

in which their aid was sought against the Dutch. The
Court also, in violation of the Treaty of 1766, required the
Company to apply for permission to peel cinnamon in the
Kandyan territory; and, on this demand being refused,
the Disāwas placed themselves at the head of their levies.
The Company's troops were now encamped at Sītāwaka.
In May the Governor went thither for the purpose of
enforcing the collection of the cinnamon. This step was
successful, and only in Sabaragamuwa was it found
necessary to support the peelers with a detachment.
Disappointed at the failure of the French and compelled
by scarcity of salt the king reopened the frontier, and
though hostilities were expected on his part on the receipt
of two threatening letters in 1792, peace continued un-
broken until the loss of Ceylon by the Dutch.

Agriculture always was actively encouraged by the
Company. The planting of coffee received attention in
1720 and of pepper in 1753. Cinnamon grew wild, and
the Dutch depended for much of the supply on the king's
country. Until the treaty of 1766 permission to collect
was only obtained by a yearly embassy, accompanied by
humiliating ceremonial, and contact with the Kandyans
led to constant trouble on the part of the peelers, but it
was only in 1769 that Falck made an attempt to cultivate
the plant at Maradāna. Though successful, it was not
until 1793 that a serious effort was made to render the
Company independent of the king for its supply. Paddy
cultivation was not lost sight of ; in 1767 the Government
attempted to reclaim the old Muturājawela fields lying to
the north of Colombo. These had been ruined by salt
water introduced by a canal, which according to De
Queyroz was constructed between Negombo and Kōttē
by a Sinhalese king, apparently Parākrama Bāhu VIII. ;
by the Dutch this canal was attributed to the Portuguese,

and was said to have been cut only some way from the Negombo lagoon. The Dutch themselves followed their custom in the Netherlands, and the numerous canals intersecting the country between Negombo and Kalutara are, with the Roman-Dutch law and the forts, the principal monument to their rule in Ceylon. A census made in 1789 gave the inhabitants of the Company's territories as numbering 817,000. The Company's prosperity, however, was waning. The European wars necessitated a large military establishment and several mercenary regiments, such as those of Wurtemburg, Luxemburg and De Meuron, were maintained at considerable expense. At the same time

FIG. 32.—Dutch Stuiver, 1783.

the Company's finances were in a precarious state ; the local currency had long been confined to copper coin, which in the absence of gold and silver became the standard, and the American war was followed by the introduction of paper money. And, further, the servants of the Company had become lethargic and no longer displayed the energy of their predecessors in the seventeenth century.

Van de Graaff was succeeded by Van Angelbeek on January 10, 1794, and in December of that year the French revolutionaries entered the Netherlands and established the Batavian Republic. The Hereditary Stadtholder fled to England and found a refuge at Kew.

THE DUTCH COMPANY.

The United East India Company was incorporated in 1602. Its organization at one time was the admiration of other nations, who used it as their model.

The shareholders formed the Assemblies or ' Chambers '

of Amsterdam, Zeeland, Delft, Rotterdam, Hoorn, and Enkhuizen, and appointed the ' Seventeen ' or Directors of the Company. These in their turn on behalf of the States General nominated the Governor-General and Council of India, and confirmed the appointments of the Company's servants provisionally made in the East. From 1748 until the establishment of the Batavian Republic the Stadtholder became the Chief Director and Governor-General-in-Chief of India, and in this capacity presided over the meetings of the Seventeen.

The administration of the Company's factories and possessions in the East was in the hands of the Governor-General and his Council. The service was divided into the Political, the Military, and the Naval branches. The grades in the Political or, as we should style it, the Civil Service were Opperkoopman (Senior Merchant), Koopman (Merchant), Onderkoopman (Junior Merchant), Boekhouder (Book-keeper), Assistant Boekhouder, Junior Assistant Boekhouder, and Aanquikeling or Zoldaat by de pen (Writer). The Military ranks were those of Major, Captain, Captain-Lieutenant, Lieutenant, Ensign, Sergeant, Corporal and Private ; and the Naval Capitan der Zee (Sea Captain), Lieutenant der Zee, and mattroos (sailor). The Equipagie Meester corresponded with our Master Attendant. There were also a considerable number of Ambachtslieden or artisans. The Ecclesiastical offices were those of Predikant and Krankbezoeker (visitor to the sick).

The Government of Ceylon was entrusted to the Governor and Director of the Island, always a member of the Council of India, and to the Political Council, consisting of the Hoofd Administrateur (Controller of Revenue), the Disāwa of Colombo, the chief military officer, the Fiscal (Public Prosecutor), and five others, the heads of the principal departments at headquarters. These were the Secretariat under the Political Secretary, the Negotie Kantoor (Trade Office), the Zoldij Kantoor (Pay Office), and the Warehouses. The Visitateur or head of the Visitie Kantoor (Audit Office) had no seat on the Council. The Dutch territories were divided between Colombo, Jaffna and Galle. The jurisdiction of Colombo extended from Kalpitiya on the north to the Bentota River on the south, and was under the Disāwa, with Opperhoofds at Kalpitiya, Negombo and Kalutara. The Captain of the Mahabadda or Cinnamon Department was subordinate to the Disāwa, who in later times held the office in addition to his own. Jaffna and Galle being at a distance from the seat of government were administered by Commandeurs, assisted by a Council. At Jaffna there was also a Disāwa, and Opperhoofds at Mannar, Trincomalee and Batticaloa. At Galle the Disāwa of Mātara was the senior member of the local Council ; the Galle Kōralē was governed by a Superintendent, who also was Captain of the Mahabadda. All these officers were Dutchmen.

The Dutch retained the old system of government inherited from the native kings by the Portuguese. The Mudaliyār assisted by Muhandirams and Ārachchis commanded the Lascorins or native militia ; the Kōrāla was in charge of the remainder of the people. Governor Falck, however, modified this arrangement in view of the disputes between the two sets of headmen by amalgamating the offices of Mudaliyār and Kōrāla. Most lands were held by service tenure, and the headmen were paid by grants of land enjoyed only while they held office. The number of offices and the extent of the land assigned to each was cut down by Van Gollenesse. The Moors and Chetties, being considered foreigners, were subject to Ūliyam or forced labour, which however could be commuted for a

cash payment.   The Malays, imported by the Dutch from
the Archipelago, were bound to military service.

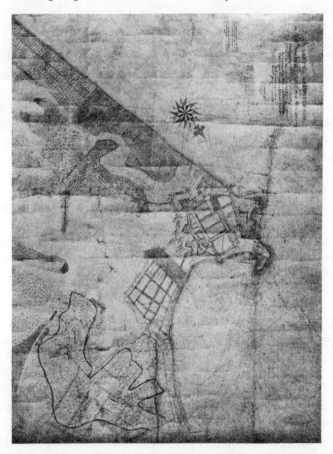

FIG. 33.—Map of Colombo, 1785.

At Colombo the chief court was (1) the Raad van
Justitie, consisting of members chosen from the Political
Council and presided over by the Hoofd Administrateur.

It had exclusive criminal jurisdiction and original jurisdiction in civil cases between Europeans and natives in Colombo : it was also a court of appeal.   (2) The Landraad dealt with litigation touching land among the natives : it was composed of the Disāwa as President, a few members of the Political Service and native chiefs. (3) The Civiel Raad or Court of Small Causes took cognizance of civil cases under 120 rixdollars in value, and had jurisdiction over Europeans and natives.   A similar Raad van Justitie under the Commandeur existed at Jaffna and Galle as well as Landraads, which also were instituted at the smaller stations.   Appeals lay from the Raads van Justitie of Jaffna and Galle and from all minor courts in civil and criminal matters to the Raad van Justitie at Colombo, and in certain cases to the Raad van Justitie at Batavia.

The Dutch Reformed Church followed the civil divisions, and a Kerkraad or Consistory was established at Colombo, Jaffna and Galle.   The staff consisted of European ministers, Native Proponents or preachers usually qualified in the Colombo Seminary, European Krankbezoekers who visited the hospitals and taught orphans, and native Catechists and Schoolmasters.   They were much exercised over the suppression of Buddhism and ' Popery.'   Education almost entirely lay in their hands.   The schools in the countryside mainly taught the Catechism and prayers, as well as reading and writing in the vernacular ; each school had from two to four teachers and every ten a Catechist.   They were supervised by the Scholarchal Commission, which in Colombo consisted of the Disāwa, the clergy of the place, and three or four members of the Political service, all nominated by the Governor.   Similar bodies existed at Jaffna and Galle.   These boards not only visited the schools yearly, but took cognizance of native

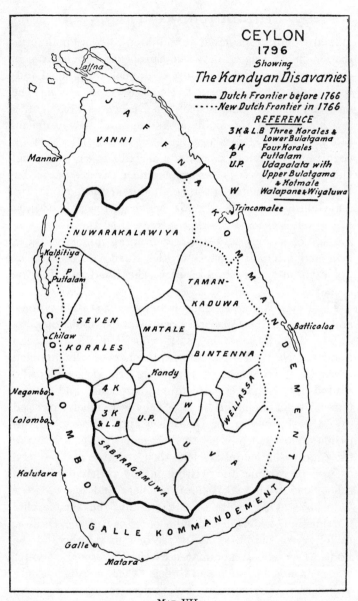

MAP VII.

marriages, issued marriage licences, and examined and appointed the schoolmasters and Tombo-holders or registrars. In 1788 the number of schools between Kalpitiya and Bentota was fifty-five. There were also elementary Dutch schools for Europeans, about seventeen in all. They were classified as Orphan, Parish, and Private : those of the first two categories were supported by the Government. Secondary education was confined to the Colombo Seminary, apparently not entirely under the control of the Scholarchal Commission ; it is first noticed in 1708. The higher course of instruction was given in Dutch. At a later date, Latin, Greek and Hebrew were added to the curriculum. The institution was mainly intended for the education of the clergy, schoolmasters and catechists. It was responsible for the translation of the whole of the New Testament and a great part of the Old into the vernacular. In 1747 a native school called the New Seminary was started in Colombo, but seems to have had no long existence. The Jaffna Seminary, begun in 1690, was discontinued in 1723.

AUTHORITIES FOR CHAPTER IX

For general history see *Beknopte Historie, Baldaeus, Valentyn, Oud en Nieuw Oost Indien*, vol. v. ; *Report on the Dutch Archives*, R. G. Anthonisz, Colombo, 1907 ; *Instructions from the Governor General and Council of India*, 1656-1665, Sophia Pieters, Colombo, 1908 ; *Memoirs* of various Dutch Governors and Commandeurs, Government Press, Colombo ; P. E. Pieris, *Ceylon and the Hollanders*, 1918, written from the Sinhalese point of view.

For the resolution to re-people part of the country see *Instructions*, pp. 17, 18. The date 1685 for the Hendala Leper Asylum is given by Van Geer ; Anthonisz attributes the completion of the building to Governor Becker, 1708.

The date of the foundation of Maha Dēwālē is given in a Sinhalese verse.

For the grievances of Van Domburg's time see Van Imhoff's secret dispatches to Batavia dated August 7 and September 26, 1736 (*Archives*, 49 D) ; for the Watubadda, also *Memoir of H. Becker*, p. 25, and *Memoir of Van Imhoff*, p. 46, and for the question of chenas, Becker's *Memoir*, p. 42.

The yacht was granted by Resolution of Council, June 20, 1740. The embassy in Dhanus, Saka 1663 = November-December 1741 is mentioned in a Sinhalese book of dates. For the death of Srī Vijaya and for the accession of Kīrti Srī and his coronation see *C.A.* ii. p. 156. It is difficult to reconcile the authorities as to the dates of the various embassies for the purpose of obtaining priests ; thus :

Dutch.	Sinhalese.
June 1740 Grant of a yacht.	
— —	Nov.-Dec. 1741, embassy starts for Siam.
1745 refusal of a vessel.	A.B. 2288 (1745/6) embassy.
1747 Vessel granted.	—

See also ' An Account of King Kirti Sri's Embassy to Siam,' *J.R.A.S.*, *C.B.*, xviii. No. 54.

For the persecution of the Catholics see *Vida do Veneravel Padre Joseph Vaz*, Lisbon, 1747.

For Schreuder's policy see Resolution of Council of August 4, 1758 (*Colombo Archives*, vol. D 113).

For the conspiracy against the king's life see ' The Moladande Rebellion,' *C.A.* ii. p. 272.

For Van Eck's expedition see *J.R.A.S.*, *C.B.* xvi. No. 50 ; for the treaty, *ib.*, and *Report on the Dutch Records*, p. 133 ; for the evacuation of the Kandy garrison, letter of Majors Frankena and Duflo, received September 10, 1765, referred to in Secret Resolution of Council of September 12 (*Archives*, D 248).

For the operations at Trincomalee in 1782 see *Ceylon Literary Register*, 1889, vol. iv. pp. 125 ff. For Van de Graaff and the Court see *Colombo Archives*, vols. D 259 (August 14, 1792), and D 261 *passim*. For Parākrama Bāhu's canal see *De Q. p.* 20 ; for the Dutch account, Resolution of Council of June 3, 1767 (D 139). For the Company's organization see *Report on the Dutch Records*, pp. 6 ff. and 125 ff. For the military, *J.R.A.S., C.B.* x. No. 37 ; for the Church and Schools, *ib.* i. (2). Bandanese assisted at the capture of Colombo and Mannar ; Javanese were allotted land at Wolvendaal (Nossa Senhora de Guadalupe) by Ryklof van Goens the Elder for military service (Resolutions of Council, September 8, 1660). For the judicial arrangements see ' Notes from Cleghorn's Minute,' *Ceylon Literary Register*, vi. 1891/2, pp. 43, 50. The Gospels were translated into Sinhalese in 1739 and into Tamil in 1743 ; the New Testament into Sinhalese in 1771-1780, and into Tamil in 1759 ; and the Pentateuch into the last-named tongue in 1790.

CHAPTER X

THE BRITISH ADMINISTRATION, 1796-1805

THE Prince of Orange had issued instructions from Kew to the Dutch Colonies to permit the entrance of British troops and ships of war for the purpose of preventing them falling into the hands of the French republicans, and orders were given to the military to use force should they be refused admittance. Accordingly in July 1795 Lord Hobart, Governor of Fort St. George, invited Governor van Angelbeek to place his colony in the possession of the British, to be restored to the Dutch at the general peace, at the same time threatening force in case of resistance. The local Dutch Government, understanding that the subversion of the old constitution of the Netherlands had been the sole work of the French, decided to adhere to the Stadtholder, but to defend themselves at Colombo, Galle, and Trincomalee if the British attempted hostilities. To Lord Hobart the Council acknowledged the British as their ' close and intimate allies,' and were prepared to receive 800 European troops, for which, however, they were not then in a position to pay, but were not ready to put the Dutch settlements under the protection of His Britannic Majesty, such a course not being required by the letter of the Prince of Orange.

The proposals of the Council were accepted by Lord Hobart, and the British forces arrived at Trincomalee. But difficulties were made by the local commandant, and the British officers reverted to their instructions and required the delivery of the forts. This was on August 2 ; the demand was refused, and the British landed unopposed but took no further steps for the moment. In the meanwhile the Dutch at Colombo had learnt that the revolution at home had been effected not by the French alone but by the majority of the nation, and in consequence decided to acknowledge the Batavian Republic, to break off all engagements with the British, and to defend the fortress to the last. This decision was communicated by letter dated August 15, 1795, to the British, who now proceeded to action at Trincomalee. The forts at this place capitulated to Colonel Steuart after a bombardment on August 28 and 31, Batticaloa fell on September 18, and Jaffna without resistance ten days later.

From Trincomalee Robert Andrews, a civilian in the Madras service, was sent as ambassador to Kandy. He returned to India with a Kandyan embassy under Mīgastennē Disāwa, and in February 1796 a treaty was signed at Madras, by which the Court was to possess a situation on the coast of Ceylon for the sole purpose of securing salt and fish, and, further, to have ten vessels free from all inspection and duty. Andrews returned to Kandy to obtain the royal signature, but the terms, which gave to the Court what it had in vain attempted to get from the Dutch, were rejected. The opportunity, once lost, did not recur.

The Count de Meuron by a provisional agreement signed at Neuchatel on March 30, 1795, had arranged for the transfer of his proprietary regiment, of which five companies were in Colombo, to the British service ; the discharge from the Dutch employ actually was effected on October 13. The Madras Government, after the fall of Jaffna, had offered once more their original conditions, but these were refused by the Dutch, who concentrated their soldiers in Colombo and prepared to defend the capital to the last. The British troops coasted along the west of Ceylon as far as Negombo, whence they advanced by land, reaching the Kelani River on February 8 and 9 without any opposition. The Dutch made no attempt to withstand the invaders between Negombo and the Kelani owing, it is said, to the advance of the Kandyans ; they intended to resist at the river, but again withdrew to Grand Pass, and the British crossed on February 11. They were attacked by the French Lieutenant-Colonel Raymond, late of the Luxemburg Regiment, next day, but occupied the Pettah. The failure of the Dutch to make a stand at the river is explained partly by the fact that the British held the sea and could have landed troops in their rear.

The Dutch Government, which in October had resolved to resist to the last, had at its disposal 1617 men, composed of 845 Europeans and 772 Malays. The British not only possessed troops to the number of 5500, of whom 2700 were Europeans, but also had command of the sea. The

Dutch had been in expectation of help from the Netherlands and Batavia and of the arrival of a French fleet, and had also hoped that Tipu Sultan of Mysore would have made a diversion in their favour. They must have realised at an early stage that resistance was hopeless ; all the staff officers, with the exception of one, and the whole of the Council were in favour of capitulation, by which private property as well as pensions to public servants would be preserved. Accordingly negotiations were commenced on the British summoning the fortress, and Colombo was surrendered on February 15, 1796 ; the terms cast no obligation on the British to restore Ceylon to the Dutch at the peace, though at the time it was anticipated that this would be done. The Dutch Governor Van Angelbeek has been charged with treason, and the failure to make any resistance, which contrasts so unfavourably with the desperate fight of the Portuguese against overwhelming numbers in 1656, lent colour to the accusation. But the documents themselves show that defence was contemplated until the position was seen to be untenable. Jacobinism is said to have been rife among the garrison, but has not been shown to have been the cause of the surrender.

The Maritime Provinces of Ceylon were now in the possession of the British. The first Englishman who is known to have lived in the Island was the Franciscan friar Andrew, who laboured in the North and lost his life there at the hands of the Hindus in 1627 or 1628. Another was the master gunner in the Kandyan service who was killed at the ' Great Stockade ' in 1632. Ralph Fitch had touched at Ceylon early in 1589, and James Lancaster in 1592. But the Englishman best known is Robert Knox, who with his father, the captain of the *Ann*, and her crew was taken prisoner by the Kandyans in 1659, and after a captivity of twenty years escaped with one companion in 1679 : he has left us a most complete and accurate account of the interior of the country.

The British settlements were attached to the Madras Presidency and administered by the East India Company through military governors. The first was Colonel (later Major-General) Steuart ; his successors were Major-General W. E. Doyle, who governed for a few months from January 1, 1797, and Brigadier-General de Meuron. Their jurisdiction was both civil and military. Towards the end of 1795 Robert Andrews was appointed Resident and Superintendent of Revenue ; under him were Collectors with Madrasi subordinates. Courts-martial dealt with cases of felony and murder, other matters coming before the Collectors. The Madras administration proved a failure. The chief causes were : (1) the supersession of the natives of the country by foreign Madrasis, who were followed by swarms of Tamils in the hope of farming the revenues ; (2) the subjection of each coconut tree as from September 1, 1796, to a yearly tax of one silver fanam, an impost sometimes in excess of the value of the produce ; (3) the abolition of the ancient service-tenure of land, which was replaced by a tax of one-tenth of the paddy crop ; and (4) the ' union of powers of renter and magistrate.' It was reported that the ' Revenue can only be collected at the point of the bayonet.' A Committee under De Meuron was appointed in June 1797 to investigate these and other matters, but, before it had time to take action, the whole country burst into violent revolt, which only came to an end early the next year. The Committee recommended the banishment of the Madrasis, the abolition of the obnoxious tax, the restoration of service-tenure and of the authority of the native chiefs, and lastly the institution of a mild and upright administration.

On October 12, 1798, the Hon. Frederic North assumed the Government. He was the first civil Governor and Commander-in-Chief and was appointed by the king, though the administration continued to be subject to the Company. The change seems to have been due to a decision to take Ceylon under the king's own authority, in view of the delay in settling with the Dutch. North's period of Government was marked by many experiments. At first the Governor was assisted by no Council ; he was the Treasurer and also the President of the Supreme Court of Criminal Jurisdiction, and of the Greater and Lesser Courts of Appeal in civil cases. In 1800 and 1801 there was instituted for lesser criminal offences and petty civil cases the Fiscal's Court, consisting of three members, while for civil cases the Landraads were reconstituted outside Colombo, Galle and Jaffna, in which towns a Civil Court was set up. By the Charter of April 18, 1801, the Supreme Court, with its jurisdiction at first confined to Colombo District, was constituted in place of the old Supreme Court of Criminal Jurisdiction in that district, and of the Civil Court of Colombo ; the High Court of Appeal consisted of the Governor, the Chief Justice, the Puisne Justice, and the Secretary to Government. In the same year the Landraads of Galle and Jaffna were abolished in favour of the Civil Courts, a measure followed up in 1802 by the merging of all the remaining Landraads into the Civil Courts, or with each other into Provincial Courts. The Fiscal's Court now was called the Court of Justices of the Peace, one of whom sat daily and was styled the Sitting Magistrate. In 1810 the jurisdiction of the Supreme Court set up in 1801 was extended to all the British Settlements, and the old Supreme Court of Criminal Jurisdiction, which still functioned outside the Colombo District, disappeared.

In the executive government the Collectors or Disāwas at first were retained, but about 1801 they were abolished and instead served on a Board of Revenue and Commerce : in their place a number of uncovenanted Agents of Revenue and Commerce were appointed. By the Peace of Amiens the possession of Ceylon was confirmed to the British. On January 1, 1802, their settlements in the Island became a Crown Colony, with a Council, ' His Majesty's Council on Ceylon,' consisting of the Chief Justice, the Commander-in-Chief and the Chief Secretary, and with a new Civil Service, that now existing. This service is the oldest in the East under the Crown. The constitution remained substantially in this state until 1833.

Education had been neglected by the military Governors but was revived by North, who followed the lines of the Dutch : in 1801 there were 170 schools. The school-masters also were Notaries and Registrars. In addition there was an Academy at Colombo with three preparatory schools.

Service-tenure had been reverted to by North on the recommendation of the Committee of Investigation, but in 1800 the Governor had come to the conclusion that abolition of the system was desirable in view of its abuse by the headmen, and of the fact that the land so held formed an inadequate remuneration for the services performed : at the same time he was of opinion that its discontinuance would result in the encouragement of agriculture and commerce as well as in the increase of revenue. Accordingly he sanctioned an optional scheme, of which he hoped that the people would take advantage. This proved a failure, and on May 1, 1802, the old system was abolished, a tax in the form of a share of the produce being substituted and personal service being enforced but paid for.

The chief sources of revenue were the Pearl Fishery, the monopoly of cinnamon, arrack, for which the principal market was in India, the duty on areca nuts, salt, tobacco, and the Ūliyam tax on the Moors in lieu of personal labour, which had been discontinued by the Madras administration but was reimposed by the Secretary of State in 1802. An impost, which caused some trouble, partly through Kandyan intrigue, was the quaintly termed Joy tax on jewels instituted in 1800.

We must now turn to North's foreign policy, which reflects very little credit on him. On July 26, 1798, Rājādhirājasinha died and was succeeded by a youthful relative, who was set on the throne by the First Adigar, Pilama Talauwē, under the name of Srī Vikrama Rājasinha (1798-1815). Muttusāmi, brother of one of the queens dowager, a member of the rival faction, fled to British territory, and was accorded a refuge at Jaffna. In February 1799 North had an interview at Avissāwēlla with Pilama Talauwē, whose object was to sound the Governor before developing his plans. At a second interview in December the Adigar directly requested the Governor to assist him in taking away the king's life and placing himself on the throne, in return for which he would make the English masters of the country. The overtures of the Adigar quite properly were rejected, and the Governor should have broken off all communication with the disloyal minister of a king with whom he was at peace. North seems to have been misled as to the extent of Pilama Talauwē's influence in the interior ; he clearly regarded the Adigar as the real power ruling through an unpopular foreign puppet. In January 1800 a further conference took place between Boyd, the acting Secretary to Government, and the Adigar, who was informed that the Governor desired the continuance of the minister's power, and would secure it to him provided that the king placed himself and his country under British protection and admitted a garrison into the capital. The safety of the king's person and the continuance of his dignity were stipulated and the question of an embassy broached. Later on the Adigar again urged the deposition of the king, to which North refused to agree as he had recognized him and had received no offence. The Governor's proposal was that the king should remove himself and his court to British territory, the Adigar ruling as his deputy at Kandy; he was only willing to send an embassy provided that the king consented to its being accompanied by a sufficient military force. This embassy he pressed for from a desire ' to elude the arts of the Adikar,' whom by this time he must have felt to be his superior in oriental diplomacy. At an interview between Boyd and the Adigar on February 1, the minister renounced all attempts on the king's life. It was clear that the Adigar expected the troops accompanying the embassy to take Kandy. But by March 4 he must have been certain that the king would not allow the entrance of so large a force into the capital, and enquired what would be considered by the Governor sufficient aggression on the part of the Kandyans to involve the two parties in war : he was then told plainly that he himself would be considered the instigator of such hostile action.

On March 12 the embassy under General Macdowall set out, but, if its object was to seize Kandy, was a failure from the beginning, as a large part of the escort was stopped at Ruwanwella. Srī Vikrama refused the treaty, in particular the articles by which the Governor undertook to send troops to Kandy whenever deemed necessary for the security of the king's throne, and counter-proposals were put forward by the Court, among them one on the subject of the ten ships, the very claim so foolishly rejected in 1796. The suggestion that the king should live in British territory does not seem to have been made. Later on the Kandyans through the chief Lewukē, one of the Adigar's enemies, once more tried to secure an establishment on the seacoast, but without success.

In February 1802 an embassy from Kandy under the Second Adigar Mīgastennē was received at Colombo, and demanded the cession of three small islands as well as the right to ten ships. Privately the ambassador renewed Pilama Talauwē's proposals to dethrone the king, but North declined to listen to him. The First Adigar also was refused an interview until he should convince the Governor of his sincerity. Accordingly he resolved to involve the king and the British in hostilities. In April thirty or forty British subjects, Moors from Puttalam, were forcibly detained, ill-treated, and robbed at the instigation of the Adigar, whose agent sold the stolen areca nuts. Demands for reparation were made to the Court, but were put off time after time until 1803, when the Governor decided to enforce the claim by arms and to exact security against a repetition of the offence. Due notice was given to the king and the Adigar and terms of settlement proposed, but without effect.

The British forces set out from Colombo on January 31, 1803, under General Macdowall, and from Trincomalee under Lieutenant-Colonel Barbut, and occupied Kandy on February 21. Barbut had found that Prince Muttusāmi, who claimed the throne and had fled to British territory in 1798, was well received on the north and east frontiers of the kingdom. Accordingly the pretender was brought to the capital and crowned on March 8, when he entered into a treaty with the Governor. By this compact the Seven Kōrales, the forts of Girihāgama and Galagedara

in Tumpanē on the present Kurunēgala-Kandy road, and
the road to Trincomalee were to be ceded to the British ;
the new king was to enter into no relations with foreign
powers save with the consent of the Ceylon Government ;
he was to pay for British troops, if required for his support,
and also provide a pension for ' the prince lately on the
throne ' ; a British minister was to reside at the Court,
when so required ; finally, the frontier duties were to be
abolished and free trade established between the interior
and the Maritime Provinces. In short, the treaty was
intended to reduce the Kandyan kingdom to the position
of a British protectorate. But Muttusāmi had no following
in the neighbourhood of Kandy, Srī Vikrama was still at
large, and his capture was the object of a fruitless expedition to Hanguranketa, undertaken at the instance of
Pilama Talauwē. On March 28 a conference was held
between Macdowall, Muttusāmi, and the Second Adigar,
at which it was agreed that Srī Vikrama should be delivered to Government and Pilama Talauwē invested with
supreme authority, paying an annuity to Muttusāmi, who
should hold his court at Jaffna. The cession of Fort
Macdowall (at the present town of Mātalē) with its surrounding district was substituted for that of Girihāgama,
the treaty to come into force as soon as Srī Vikrama was
in the hands of the British. Meanwhile there was to be
an immediate cessation of hostilities.

On April 1 General Macdowall departed from Kandy,
leaving a garrison under Barbut ; great loss had occurred
through disease, and its safety entirely depended on the
good faith of the Adigar. His power was not such as
North imagined, and hostilities were continued by the
chiefs. On May 5 North met Pilama Talauwē at
Dambadeniya, in the newly ceded Seven Kōralēs, and
the treaty of March 28 was confirmed. It afterwards

transpired that the Adigar had intended to kidnap the Governor, who was saved by the timely appearance of Barbut from Kandy. This officer died on May 21, and the command of the Kandy garrison devolved upon Major Davie, an officer whose capacity and experience were quite unequal to the situation. Macdowall was requested by the Adigar again to come to Kandy. This he did on

FIG. 34.—Meeting of General Macdowall and Pilama Talauwē.
1. General Macdowall.   2. Pilama Talauwē.   3. The Moodliar Interpreter.

May 23, but, the minister failing to appear, left the capital for the last time, sick with fever, on June 11. The garrison, left to its fate, was closely blockaded : the Europeans were dying at the rate of six a day, and 450 out of the 700 Malays deserted. On June 24 the Kandyans attacked but were repulsed. Davie now was persuaded by his officers that further resistance was impossible, and the garrison capitulated on the condition that the able bodied should march with their arms to Trincomalee with Muttusāmi, and that the Adigar should care for the sick and wounded until they could be removed. Unfortunately the Mahaweliganga was in flood. The king now having the troops at his mercy, demanded the surrender of Muttusāmi, who was basely given up and was at once killed, and then ordered the return of the soldiers unarmed to Kandy. Once their arms were laid down a general massacre ensued on June 26 at ' Davie's Tree ' on the outskirts of Kandy. The sick and wounded already had been butchered. The one redeeming feature of this sordid affair was the constancy of the Malay officer Nūruddīn and his brother, who refusing to abandon the British service were murdered at Hanguranketa. Captain Madge of Fort Macdowall, hearing of the massacre, retreated to Trincomalee : the post of Dambadeniya successfully held out against the Second Adigar until relieved from Colombo. The ill-conceived expedition, undertaken by North in reliance on the good faith of Pilama Talauwē, whom the Governor knew to be thoroughly unscrupulous, thus ended in utter disaster : many lives had been lost ; the hospitals were crowded, and a very large number succumbed to the diseases contracted during the campaign. The king was victorious, but the massacre was fatal to the continued existence of the Kandyan kingdom.

Towards the end of July the Kandyans were threatening the frontiers, and in August and September invaded the British territories in all directions, prevailing upon many of the natives to join them. The enemy advanced within fourteen or fifteen miles of Colombo, and on August 21 took the small fort of Hanwella ; this was shortly afterwards recovered and the Kandyans driven back to Sītāwaka. The king, however, with the usual ignorance of the outside world characterizing the Kandyan Court, hoped to take Colombo with a few six-pounder guns, and again early in September attacked the fort of Hanwella, defended by invalids.   But on September 6 he was completely routed, and retreated, never stopping in his flight until safe within his own dominions : Lewukē, who was unfortunate enough to overtake the fugitive, paid for his temerity with his life.   In this action the British recovered 150 Bengal and Madras lascars, who had been pressed into the Kandyan service and took this opportunity to desert. After this hostilities were confined to incursions into the king's territory, with instructions to lay it waste, until the arrival of fresh reinforcements.   General Wemyss relieved Macdowall in February 1804, and a concerted attack from all sides was proposed with the object of causing ' the greatest devastation and injury to the enemy's country,' the troops to meet in Kandy on September 28 and 29.   The expedition, however, was countermanded, but with such lack of clearness in the instructions that Captain Johnston set out from Batticaloa, occupied Kandy, and finding himself unsupported fought his way to Trincomalee, with a force of eighty-two Europeans and 202 sepoys.   Of these he lost in killed and wounded seventy-one, but of the rest few survived owing to sickness. Desultory war continued, martial law being in force in the British territories, until February 1805, when an extensive invasion by the Kandyans took place.   Their only success, however, was the surprise of the small frontier fort of Katuwana.   After this the British received large reinforcements, the king had smallpox, and a tacit suspension of hostilities ensued owing to the exhaustion of the Kandyans.

Nothing can be said for North's weak and vacillating policy, if indeed he had a policy ; it was not even justified by success.   He doubtless shared Wellesley's idea of elevating the British Government to a position of paramount power in India, and does not seem to have been particular as to the means adopted. He clearly had little reliable information touching Pilama Talauwē's position in the Kandyan country or the king's power, but he was well aware of the Adigar's character ; yet he staked the success of the expedition of 1803 upon that minister's good faith. The only honest policy to have been adopted was an absolute refusal to enter into the Adigar's intrigues at the outset. Pilama Talauwē's policy throughout was consistent, namely to depose the foreign dynasty and to make himself supreme ;

but he was not strong enough to overcome the jealousy of the other chiefs, and the king showed more ability than he credited him for pos-

FIG. 35.—British Stuiver, 1801.

sessing. The British Government to the Adigar merely was a tool, to be discarded once he was on the throne, but he does not seem to have been responsible for the massacre of 1803, which was the work of the king himself.

AUTHORITIES FOR CHAPTER X

The letter of the Prince of Orange is given in the *Report on the Dutch Archives*, p. 138 ; the Prince's instructions of February 2, by which naval and military commanders were ordered ' de se mettre sous la protection de S.M.', were not received in Ceylon.

The Wellesley Manuscripts, extracts from, published in *Ceylon Literary Register*, ii. pp. 124 ff. ; *Description of Ceylon*, James Cordiner, 1807 ; *Voyages and Travels to India, Ceylon, etc.*, Lord Valentia, 1809 ; *Narrative of the Operations of a Detachment in an Expedition to Candy* . . . 1804, Major Johnston, 1810 ; *View of the Agricultural, Commercial and Financial Interests of Ceylon*, A. Bertolacci, 1817 ; *Account of the Interior*

of Ceylon, John Davy, 1821 ; *Eleven Years in Ceylon*, Major
Forbes, 1840 ; *Ceylon*, H. Marshall, 1846 ; *Ceylon*, Sir James
Emerson Tennent, 1859 ; *Collected Papers on the History of
the Maritime Provinces of Ceylon*, 1795-1805, L. J. B. Turner,
1923 ; ' Pilama Talawuwe, Maha Adigar : his political intrigues,
1798-1803,' L. J. B. Turner, in *C.A.* iii. p. 219.

CHAPTER XI

THE BRITISH ADMINISTRATION, 1805-1833

On July 19, 1805, Sir Thomas Maitland (1805-1812),
succeeded North as Governor. No intercourse was held
with the Court of Kandy, but there was no aggression by
either party. In 1808 the Seven Kōralēs were divided by
the king in pursuance of his policy of reducing the power
of the chiefs, and Ehelēpola and Molligoda were appointed
as heads of the two provinces so formed. The new
arrangement was the cause of popular discontent, owing
to all the services being doubled, and this finally broke
out in rebellion. The rising was suppressed by Pilama
Talauwē and his son-in-law Ratwattē. But the First
Adigar's success increased the king's jealousy and suspicion
and at last he was disgraced ; he then conspired to assassinate his master, but the plot being revealed by a premature rising he was condemned to death and beheaded
in 1811. Pilama Taluwē was succeeded as First Adigar
by Ehelēpola.

In internal affairs Maitland reversed his predecessor's
land policy. The cost of the cooly corps which had been
raised to supply the labour formally rendered by the
holders of service-lands was found to exceed the revenue
obtained from these lands, and the loss to Government
was heavy. Cultivation had decreased, because of the

tax, the collection of which was vexatious to the people ; the new liberty enjoyed by them was misused, and, in consequence, crime had increased ; in short, North's policy had been premature, and accordingly the old system was re-established. Grants of lands to Europeans, save in Colombo and its district, were prohibited. By the Charter of Justice of 1811 trial by jury was extended to all British subjects. The Provincial Courts also were abolished and the Landraads revived, a measure reversed the following year. The year 1806 saw Catholics relieved of the disabilities imposed on them by the Dutch, and also the first appointment of Police Vidānēs or headmen entrusted with police duties. The apathy of Maitland in effecting Major Davie's escape is not to his credit.

Sir Robert Brownrigg (1812-1820) assumed the Government on March 11, 1812. With the exception of the establishment of the first Botanic Garden in this year there is nothing to record in the British territories, and Brownrigg's administration was entirely taken up with the Kandyan question.

In 1814 the king sent the chiefs to their districts. Among them Ehelēpola Adigar went to Sabaragamuwa, of which he was Disāwa. Complaints as to his rule reached the king, already suspicious of his minister ; Ehelēpola was summoned to Kandy, but well knowing his master's temper refused to obey and rebelled. Molligoda, succeeding to his offices, crushed the revolt, and Ehelēpola fled to British territory and safety in May. The king unable to lay his hands on the chief offender gave rein to his sanguinary temper, and executed the late Adigar's wife, infant children and other relatives, with a barbarity which shocked even the Kandyans, accustomed as they were to such spectacles. Not content with this the king again investigated the old rebellion of 1808 in the Seven Kōralēs.

But the king's cup was now full. The British Government was aware of his unpopularity with the chiefs and endeavoured to win over Molligoda. In November ten merchants, British subjects, were robbed in the Three Kōralēs, charged with espionage, and then mutilated ; seven died on the spot, and the remainder were sent to Colombo. This outrage was deemed an act of aggression and preparations were made for war, but the expedition had to be postponed for the time, as the troops asked for from Madras were recalled to India. The army, however, moved early in 1815, two divisions marching from each of the fortresses of Colombo, Galle and Trincomalee, and one each from Batticaloa and Negombo. On January 10 the first engagement took place, the Kandyans pursuing Ehelēpola's men across the Sītāwaka River into British territory, where they burnt a house. War was declared the same day, the grounds alleged being the barbarity perpetrated on the ten British subjects, the implacable animosity of the king, and his unwillingness to enter into any agreement with the Government to terminate a state of affairs so unsettled and precarious. The objects of hostilities were declared to be the permanent tranquillity of the British settlements, the vindication of the honour of the British name, the deliverance of the Kandyans from their oppressors and the subversion of the Malabar dominion. The Governor further promised to the chiefs the continuance of their dignities. The division accompanied by Brownrigg advanced through the Three and Four Kōralēs and met with little resistance. Molligoda had arranged to simulate defence, but soon in person surrendered his province of the Four Kōralēs to the Governor. Kandy was occupied on February 14, and the king himself captured by Ehelēpola's men four days later.

The royal prisoner was sent to Colombo and ultimately
to India, where he died in exile on January 30, 1832, at
the age of fifty-two. His only son died childless in 1843.
The late king had been placed on the throne in his youth
by the unscrupulous Pilama Talauwē, and for a time saw
little except through the Adigar's eyes. He soon found

FIG. 36.—Srī Vikrama Rājasinha, King of Kandy, 1798-1815.

himself confronted with intrigues to dethrone him, if not
to take his life, on the part of his minister, and though he
succeeded in freeing himself from this danger he had
become, surrounded as he was by intriguing chiefs, subject
to constant fear and suspicion, never sleeping two watches
of the night in the same room. Further, perhaps as a
result of his situation, he became addicted to drink, and

developed into a bloodthirsty despot. His punishments went beyond custom, and he even executed Buddhist priests. In his favour must be set the construction of the Kandy lake, of the Octagon and other buildings, all carried out after 1803. It must also be recorded that he defended the lower and middle classes from the exactions of the chiefs, whose power he strove to diminish. In so doing he incurred the displeasure of powerful families, and their desire to be rid of him extended to his whole house, in whose debt many of the chiefs stood. Had he not alienated these the expedition of 1815 might not have had a successful issue. As it was, in the words of the Official Declaration of the Settlement of the Kandyan Provinces ' Led by the invitation of the chiefs, and welcomed by the acclamations of the people, the forces of His Britannic Majesty have entered the Kandyan territory, and penetrated to the capital. The ruler of the interior provinces has fallen into their hands, and the government remains at the disposal of his Majesty's representative.'

The Governor acceded to the wishes of the Kandyans, and on March 2, 1815, a Convention was held at Kandy between His Excellency on the one hand and the chiefs as representing the people on the other. At this the king was deposed, his dynasty excluded from the throne, the chiefs were guaranteed the continuance of their rights and privileges, and the Buddhist religion was to be maintained. The Government of the Kandyan Provinces was vested in a Board of Commissioners, consisting of the Resident, John D'Oyly, afterwards created a Baronet for his services, the Judicial and Revenue Commissioners, and the Officer commanding the troops. These with the Adigars and principal chiefs formed the Great Court of Justice, from which there was no appeal except to the Governor.

The native system of government was retained, subject to the supervision of Agents of Government in Uva, Sabaragamuwa and the Three Kōralēs. Molligoda continued as First Adigar ; Ehelēpola had hoped to succeed to the vacant throne, and declined office.

But the new administration, after all a foreign one, was not popular. The people for generations had been accustomed to corruption, and the very fact of even justice regardless of caste and privilege was an offence. The chiefs in particular were affected as, though the old system was scrupulously maintained, in practice they were subordinate to the Agents of Government and to every military officer. Individually the British were not disliked, but there was no bond of sympathy, particularly in the matter of religion, and the wish was general that the foreigner, having ridded the Kandyans of a tyrant, should return whence he came. The chiefs even in 1815 were not credited with sincerity in signing the Convention. Ehelēpola in particular, having failed to secure the crown for himself, was discontented. But in this lay safety for the new administration. The chiefs, at least for a time, preferred the British to Ehelēpola ; they were not prepared to submit to the royal authority wielded by an equal, and the usual jealousy prevailing among them prevented any formidable conspiracy to oust the British by force of arms. When the outburst came it was due to accidental causes.

The rebellion broke out in Wellassa. The local Moors had been put under a separate headman of their own race, and the Sinhalese of the district were discontented. In September 1817 a strange priest appeared in the jungle, and Wilson, the Assistant Resident at Badulla, sent a party of Moors to arrest him. Resistance was offered ; Wilson found the country in opposition to authority, the priest posing as a member of the royal family, and he was murdered on September 16. The revolt spread to Uva and Walapanē, and Keppitipola, Disāwa of Uva, sent to put down the movement, joined the rebels. The flame spread, 'uniformity of feeling supplying the place of organization,' until on February 21, 1818, all the Kandyan Provinces were placed under martial law. By the next month the only districts remaining loyal to the Government were the lower part of Sabaragamuwa, the Three and Four Kōralēs, and two small divisions near Kandy : every chief of note, with the exception of Molligoda, was in rebellion or in prison, including Ehelēpola himself, who was arrested on March 3. The position was so serious that it is alleged that at one time arrangements were made for withdrawal from the interior. The situation was saved by Molligoda's loyalty, by which the road to Kandy was kept open ; he was the enemy of Ehelēpola, and he identified British rule with his own safety. The issue was still doubtful in May, June and July : but during the next two months the troops were chiefly occupied in pursuing fugitive chiefs. At the end of August Madugallē joined the pretender and became his Second Adigar, but soon discovered that he was an ex-priest known as Wilbāwē ; he thereupon imprisoned the impostor as well as Keppitipola. Wilbāwē, however, after his exposure was released and disappeared, succeeding in escaping capture by the British until 1829. The people began to realize that they had nothing to gain from continued resistance except famine, and hostilities abated. On October 30 Keppitipola was captured, and on November 1 Madugallē. The rebellion now collapsed. The two ringleaders were beheaded on November 26. Ehelēpola remained in Colombo until 1825, when he was sent to Mauritius ; he died there in April, 1829, aged fifty-six.

The suppression of the rebellion entailed great devastation, especially in Uva. On the British side the mortality among the troops, chiefly due to sickness, amounted nearly to 25 per cent. The principal political result was the alteration of the government in the interior. The Convention of 1815 had been deliberately broken by the Kandyans, and Government, having found by experience the difficulty of working the ancient system, accordingly abolished the old land tenure, reserving personal services save in a few cases only for work on the roads and bridges ; in their place it imposed a tax payable in a share of the paddy crop, and further put the administration of the country in the hands of British officers. The temples continued on the old footing, the appointment of the chief priests and the lay headmen remaining as before with the Crown. Government also reserved to itself the right to make such further alterations as might appear necessary. On February 12, 1819, martial law ceased in the Kandyan Provinces, and the peace was not afterwards broken save by short disturbances in 1820, 1823 and 1824.[1]

From February 1, 1820, the government was administered by Sir Edward Barnes as Lieutenant-Governor. The next year the road from Kurunēgala to Kandy was opened. Lieutenant-General Sir Edward Paget became Governor on February 2, 1822. In his period of office Molligoda the elder died on October 26, 1823. On January 18 of the following year Sir Edward Barnes succeeded and continued his policy of opening communications. The present road from Colombo to Kandy was completed in 1825 ; that from Kandy northwards had reached Mātalē in 1831, Dambulla in 1832, and had been constructed as far as the boundary of Trincomalee District in 1833. Sir John D'Oyly, the Resident, died on May 25, 1824. He was

---

[1] The slight trouble in 1842-3 and the formidable rising of 1848 lie outside our period.

a Sinhalese scholar, and had such an extensive and intimate knowledge of things Kandyan that it was found impossible to find an adequate successor ; accordingly his post was not filled. It was under Barnes' administration that the cultivation of coffee was introduced into the interior. He was succeeded on October 23, 1831, by Sir Robert W. Horton (1831-1837). Since 1829 a Commission of Enquiry under Major Colebroke had been investigating the administration of the country. The result of its labours was an Order of the King in Council, proclaimed on September 28, 1833. By this compulsory labour was abolished ; the old Council of Government was dissolved, and Executive and Legislative Councils established in its place ; the separate administration of the interior was done away and the Kandyan districts amalgamated with the old British settlements on the coast, each of the new provinces being under a Government Agent. The cinnamon monopoly, which had long ceased to be profitable owing to the competition of Java and China, was also discontinued. By the Charter of Justice of August 31, 1833, a new Supreme Court was erected, and shortly afterwards District Courts were brought into being. The union of the Kandyan with the Maritime Provinces, the substitution of smaller divisions under Ratēmahatmayās for the old provinces under Disāwas, and the abolition of forced service and of compulsory attendance at festivals were not acceptable to the chiefs, and resulted in a plot against the Government led by the younger Molligoda in 1834. The conspirators were tried before the Supreme Court in 1835 but were acquitted : Molligoda, however, was dismissed and his place taken by Mahawalatennē, the last of the old line of Adigars.

With the final disappearance of a separate administration for the interior we may review the Kandyan system of government as it existed in 1815. The king was supreme, and his autocratic power was controlled only by custom and by the fear of assassination. Where the succession was doubtful, the selection of the new monarch in practice lay with the principal ministers, and their choice was formally ratified by the people, but normally son followed father on the throne. The chief Officers of State were the two Adigars, the first of whom occasionally was styled in solemn documents by the old title of Sene-virad or Commander-in-Chief : they were the royal ministers and had a general supervision over the whole kingdom. Their emoluments were few, and in consequence they always held one or more provinces with other offices for the maintenance of their dignity. For a long period of time there had been one minister, apparently the Vikramasinha ; Rājasinha II. is said to have added a second, and the last king of Kandy a third. Beneath these were the Great Disāwas or provincial governors of the Four and the Seven Kōralēs, Uva, and Mātalē, and eight minor Disāwas, but the number varied ; they usually resided at the capital, and on going to their provinces were obliged to leave their families as hostages in Kandy. The smaller districts round the capital were governed by Ratēmahatmayās, chiefs of much less importance than the Disāwas. In addition there existed a number of departments attached to the palace under chiefs styled Lēkams or Secretaries ; most of these had once been military in nature, but by the end of the eighteenth century had become little more than bodies of messengers. Certain people throughout the country by virtue of the tenure in which they held their lands were liable to military service ; they performed this duty for periods of fifteen days at a time, supplying their own weapons, portable shelters and food, and were then relieved by others. But the backbone of the military force was the small standing army, consisting chiefly of Malays, who received pay in lieu of land. By the beginning of the nineteenth century muskets practically had superseded other weapons ; the gingals were supplemented by a few cannon. Usually guerilla tactics were employed ; the enemy was allowed to enter the country, and on his return was perpetually harassed, and, if possible, entrapped in an ambush and attacked by musket and gingal fire from the cover of the forest, through which the road, a narrow track, ran. The royal villages set apart for the maintenance of the king and of the royal family were under the supervision of the Gabadā Nilamēs or chiefs of the Store Houses. All the chiefs held their office at the royal pleasure.

The administration of justice was in the hands of the chiefs and headmen, all of whom had the power of inflicting slight punishments and fines. The king alone had the power of life and death, and the Great Court consisting of the principal chiefs could only impose such punishments as were within the competence of the Adigars ; all important matters were referred to the king. In the remoter districts popular courts, probably of great antiquity, survived, and almost everywhere the village councils (gam-sabē) ; no fines could be imposed unless a headman presided, and every member present received at least a small share of the money so recovered. In the courts of the Disāwas at least great corruption prevailed, and there was no such thing as finality in a case, which could always be reopened for a bribe. The last king is said to have encouraged the old popular tribunals as a means of reducing the power of the chiefs. But these institutions in most places were already extinct or moribund, and his measures came too late. Ordeals were in common use.

All lands were held by service tenure. The chief source of the king's revenue was in the royal villages. He also received as tax rice from holders of lands other than those assigned for military service or allotted to members of particular castes organized for the performance of the duties proper thereto ; the amount so raised cannot have been considerable. The marāla or death duty has been discussed in Chapter III. Another source of income was the dekum or present from the chiefs on appointment. The king received these also at the New Year, at which festival the chiefs benefited as well, receiving presents from all the minor headmen whose turn of office only lasted for a year. The system still continues in the Kandyan temples.

The king's power was also felt in religion. The chief priests were appointed and the candidates for ordination approved by the sovereign ; the chiefships of the Tooth Relic Temple and of the principal temples of the gods were granted by him to the Adigars and others as a means of maintaining their dignity. But in no case were the extensive temple lands considered to be free from the royal supervision, and no difference was made between the administration of the properties belonging to the Tooth Relic and to the gods and that of other departments of State.

We have now reached the conclusion of this historical outline, the year 1833 having been selected as from the constitution then settled the present system of government has been gradually developed. It only remains to indicate the causes of the union of Ceylon under the British Crown, the first union achieved since the early thirteenth century. As far as we can get back to the origins, the first cause is the perpetual discord among the royal family of Kōttē. The Portuguese arrived and, as is their custom, made the king of Kōttē tributary to Portugal. But their fort was dismantled on orders from home, and it was only on the entreaty of the king that they involved themselves in war in his defence against Māyādunnē. Then their eyes were opened to the possibilities of the situation, and the result was the Donation of Dharmapāla. The assumption of the crown of Kōttē and the overlordship of Ceylon by the king of Portugal drove the native government into the interior, and this position was not altered by the arrival of the Dutch on the invitation of Rājasinha and later by the conquest of the Maritime Provinces by the British, save that the coast was now held by a stronger power. The Kandyan Court never observed any treaty obligation ; at any time it was in a position to threaten or actually invade the richer regions below the mountains, and was the centre and active cause of disaffection in the country held by the Dutch or British. The position was intolerable to a civilized government, and the natural result followed, the extinction of the restless and untrustworthy neighbour in the interior. Rights and wrongs existed on either side, but the broad outlines of history are as have been just related.

AUTHORITIES FOR CHAPTER XI

Bertolacci, Davy, Forbes, Marshall, Tennent, as in Chapter X., and ' Diary of Mr. John D'Oyly, 1810-1815,' in *J.R.A.S.*, *C.B.* xxv. No. 69. For the constitution of the Kandyan kingdom, described by D'Oyly, see *Report on the Kēgalla District*, p. 107. For Kandyan military matters see Major Johnston, *op. cit.*

CHAPTER XII

ARCHAEOLOGY

By A. M. Hocart

PREHISTORIC times are represented in Ceylon by rude implements of quartz and of chert. All those hitherto found belong to the same type : points with a triangular section, differing only in the degree of flatness. They are remarkably like many points claimed as eoliths, only there can be no doubt about the chert examples having been used by man, since they are found in places where they can only have been brought by man. The stone industry of Ceylon was distinctly less advanced in technique than even the earliest palaeolithic industries of Europe. Who used those tools, and when, we have no means of deciding.

From the Eolithic Age we jump straight to the Iron Age. We do not know when iron was introduced into Ceylon.

Cave paintings have been found near Tantrimalai, which have no connection with Indian art.

Apart from stone implements and these cave paintings the archaeology of Ceylon begins with Buddhism. Brick was doubtless known before then, but no remains have been found which there is any reason to suppose to be pre-Buddhistic. The greater glory of the Church was down to the latest times almost the only impulse to set up ambitious buildings of durable materials.

At first brick seems scarcely to have been used for hollow structures. It is difficult, however, to be positive on this point as, owing to the absence of lime mortar, any brick walls set up in this period would not have lasted.

Brick was extensively used in topes, dāgabas as they are called in Ceylon, that is relic shrines, solid hemispherical masses which have been derived by Ferguson from the round barrow with every show of reason. The first tope to be erected by a king is the Thūpārāma at Anurādhapura : it had a core of mud, and only the outer casing was of brick ; it was of moderate dimensions. Dutthagāmani set the fashion of building colossal topes of solid brick, and was emulated by Vattagāmani and Mahāsēna ; then all attempts at emulation were given up, at least in Anurādhapura, till the reign of Parākrama Bāhu, who loved the grandiose. He built the largest tope on record, but not the most durable, the Demala Maha Säya ; it is now a shapeless mass. In the intervening period small topes continued to be built with rubble core and brick casing.

This mode of construction was down to the twelfth century almost the only one used by the Sinhalese when using brick or stone, for all such structures were either topes or else square plinths of earth or rubble, with retaining walls.

At what time the Sinhalese first became acquainted with lime is not known. It was used in the sixth century at Sīgiriya, where there is some fine marble-like plaster ; but down to the twelfth century it was not extensively used, possibly because Ceylon is poor in lime, and the means of communication did not encourage the transport of shell or coral lime from the sea-coast. The Polonnaruwa kings made great use of lime, possibly because the Mahavāliganga provided a cheap and easy waterway. They were thus able to erect complete brick temples covered with massive brick vaults. This culminated in the Lankātilaka. The arch now appears, but its principle was never understood, with the result that the roofs invariably collapsed after a time. Mud mortar continued to be used for minor buildings, and as late as the fourteenth century we find mud mortar used in the Kandyan Lankātilaka, the most important building of the age.

The first appearance of stone cannot be dated with certainty, but it does not seem to be before the Christian era. It first takes the form of rows of stones forming the foundations of mud walls. About the third century low rubble retaining walls were built round square platforms of earth. These increased in height, and stones cut into irregular shapes fitting in with one another took the place of rubble. The succeeding age brought in perfectly smooth stones cut to a rectangular shape. At first these temples remained very small, and each member of each side consisted of one enormous slab. The next period increased the dimensions of the platform, introduced simple mouldings, and to some extent substituted stone for wooden pillars. The capitals, however, remained of wood, and this continued to be the custom even down to the eighteenth century, as can be seen at the Tooth Relic Temple in Kandy, although stone capitals were somewhat in fashion during the twelfth century, and perhaps a little earlier. We have now reached somewhere about the eighth century ; in the ninth or tenth stone work attained its zenith of excellence : it was rich but with taste, there was a finish about the work which was subsequently much impaired and eventually was completely lost.

Up to now the main type of hollow structure was a square or oblong house standing on a plinth, such as has been described. An idea of these buildings can be gained from the present Tooth Relic Temple, which is a lineal descendant of this type. As the whole superstructure was timber and tiles it will be understood at once why, at the present day, there is little else than plinths to be seen in

Anurādhapura and elsewhere. Some of these buildings
were shrines round which were grouped dwelling-houses,
wash-house, store-house, etc. Up to about the eighth
century the type of shrine in vogue consisted of two platforms, the shrine proper and the tomtoming hall, connected by a bridge consisting of a single enormous slab.
In the age of plain ashlar, say about the sixth century,
monastic settlements were often based on a long paved
avenue along the foot of a hill leading up to the main
tope or temple with paths leading right and left to other
buildings. Good examples of this are to be seen at
Arankäḷē near Kurunägala, and Ritigala near Habaranē.
At the time when simple mouldings came in the sub-
sidiary buildings were grouped on level ground round the
main one. The double platform disappeared in the ninth
or tenth century.

The twelfth and thirteenth centuries were, as we have
seen, ages of brickwork ; stone receded into the back-
ground. Subsequent ages were too troubled to give much
scope for big works. Special efforts in stonework were
made at Yāpahuva and Gadalādeniya. The brick temple
of Lankātilaka near Kandy has been mentioned.

The only monuments completely built of stone are
Hindu temples. The early Pallava period (seventh-eighth
century) is represented by the Gedigē at Nālanda near
Mātalē, the Chōla style (tenth-eleventh) by the Siva
Temple No. 2 at Polonnaruwa, the Pāndyan (twelfth-
fourteenth) by the Siva Temple No. 1. The Vijayanagar
style is so far missing. The Madura style has numerous
representatives of recent date in Colombo and elsewhere.

Natural cave temples are innumerable, but excavated
ones are rare ; only four examples are known so far.
There is a threefold reason for this : the hardness of the

gneiss which is almost the only rock, the multitude of natural rock shelters, and the small size of Sinhalese temples. Even the excavated caves are diminutive, affording accommodation for a statue or two and for worshippers. The hardness of the stone also accounts to a great extent for the meagre output of Ceylon sculpture. The primitive Indian school is represented by two fragments which were imported from Amarāvatī, and therefore do not really belong to Ceylon. There is also a piece in the Colombo Museum that appears to be a local production in the style of Amarāvatī (No. 46A). There are a certain number of carvings which we might assign to the early Gupta period (fourth century), in particular a pleasing group of a man and a woman at Isurumuniya. These dates, it must be remembered, are based entirely on the analogy of Indian art, as there is no external evidence. Sculpture in the round does not appear till the ninth or tenth century, and by that time Indian art had become stereotyped, so that the Ceylon artists entirely missed the inspiration of the earlier periods. Yet at the same time the stone carvers were turning out some of their best work, such as the moonstone at the so-called Queen's Pavilion in Anurādhapura, which for perfection of technique is unsurpassed in Ceylon. During the Polonnaruwa period there developed a passion for the colossal in sculpture which continues to the present day. Huge Buddhas, standing, sitting, or recumbent, were fashioned of brick-work plastered over, sometimes carved out of the rock, for instance at Galvihārē in Polonnaruwa, Kalāvāva, Tantrimalai. As works of art, however, they do not rank high. The only exception is the statue, said to be of Parākrama Bāhu the Great, at Potgul Vehera, Polonnaruwa, which stands in a class by itself ; its breadth and dignity cannot fail to impress ; the face shows no attempt at idealization, so much so that one is tempted to suppose that it is a portrait ; if so, it is almost unique in Indian art, which only tried to take an interest in portraiture under the influence of the Kushān Kings. The stone carving of the period is much inferior to that of the preceding one and has no new ideas. Stucco work on the other hand takes a great development corresponding with the efflorescence of brickwork. The artists love movement, and some of the stucco dwarfs are amusingly lively. This passion for movement led to violent exaggeration in the next age, as can be seen at Yāpahuva and elsewhere ; in their attempt at rendering the exertions of dancers the artists even distorted the anatomy ; this exaggeration disfigures an otherwise delicate little frieze of dancers from Polonnaruwa in the Colombo Museum (No. 105).   In the Kandyan period the lines are drawn without delicacy, and the artist, unable to see the beauty of straight lines or simple curves, tries to enrich his work with little ripples of drapery that merely irritate.

All buildings were plastered over.   In the Polonnaruwa period they are known to have been painted ; earlier buildings were no doubt also painted.   Nevertheless, the surviving specimens of Sinhalese paintings are few.   The oldest known are those at Sīgiriya (sixth century) representing, it would seem, divine women in the clouds.   They are isolated figures and do not appear to form a subject. The fresco at Hindagala near Kandy is assigned by experts to the seventh century : it represents the Temptation. At Polonnaruwa we have a whole series of birth stories depicted on the walls of the Northern Temple.

Excavations have not thrown a very favourable light on the crafts of Ceylon : the finds are most jejune.   The pottery remains rude to the present day ; even now the art of glazing is not known nor is the wheel in universal use. The Sinhalese were essentially an agricultural people, and their greatest achievements lie in that direction. Less is heard about their tanks, as the artificial reservoirs are called, than about their monuments, yet they are a far more outstanding performance. Minnēriya tank, one of the largest, though not the largest, when full covers 4560 acres. The channels linking tank with tank are praised by modern engineers. One expert declares that it would be hard to improve the old levels. Unfortunately the history of irrigation is difficult to trace, because even when we know the date of a tank it stands to reason that it was perpetually being repaired. As for improvements in the planning, if they exist, it requires expert knowledge to trace them. The fourth to sixth centuries appear to have been a great tank-building age : Minnēriya was built by Mahāsēna, who is now worshipped as the ' Minnēri god ' ; Kalāväva was the work of Dhātusēna, Giritalē and Kantalai of Aggabōdhi II. All these tanks have a certain family resemblance, being held up by enormous yet relatively short bunds.

The general characteristic of Sinhalese work is simplicity and small dimensions ; yet special efforts were at times put forth, resulting in colossal topes, colossal statues, and immense irrigation works.

AUTHORITIES FOR CHAPTER XII

A general survey of Ceylon Archaeology will be found in the Archaeological Summaries published annually in the *Ceylon Journal of Science*. Detailed studies of particular ruins are published in the *Memoirs of the Archaeological Survey of Ceylon*. Numerous photographs are published in the Annual Reports of the Archaeological Survey.

For primitive cave paintings see Still's ' Tantrimalai ' in *J.R.A.S., C.B.* vol. xxii.

Parker's *Ancient Ceylon* is full of information, but is to be used with caution.

The standard work on coinage is Codrington's *Ceylon Coins and Currency*.

Inscriptions are published in *Epigraphia Zeylanica*.

CHIEF EVENTS SINCE 1833

1835.   Molligoda Adigar and other Kandyans tried for high treason and acquitted.

1844.   Police Courts established.   Abolition of slavery.

1845.   Courts of Requests established.   Formation of the North Western Province.

1848.   The " Mātalē Rebellion " ; insurrection of Kandyans in Mātalē and Kurunēgala Districts.

1853.   The Government finally dissociates itself from the administration of Buddhist ecclesiastical affairs.

1858.   The first telegraph line constructed.   Inauguration of the railway.

1867.   The railway between Colombo and Kandy opened.   Ten acres planted in tea.

1869.   The Department of Public Instruction constituted.

1872.   Decimal currency introduced with the rupee as the standard coin, in lieu of sterling.

1873.   The Ceylon Rifle Regiment disbanded.   The North Central Province formed.

1875.   The Prince of Wales (King Edward VII.) lays the foundation of the Colombo breakwater.

1877.   The Colombo Museum opened.

1881.   Disestablishment of the Church of England and Presbyterians. Commencement of the Ceylon Volunteer Force.

1882.   Visit of the Princes Albert Victor and George of Wales.

1883.   The output of coffee, the planting of which was begun in 1827, reduced owing to disease by one-third.   The industry was succeeded by the planting of cinchona, and ultimately by the end of the decade by that of tea.   In this year rubber first planted on a commercial scale.

1885.   Beginning of the existing Government Note currency.

1886.   Province of Uva constituted.

1889.   Province of Sabaragamuwa formed, making the ninth province.

1892.   Paddy tax abolished.

1896.   Seacoast railway line completed to Mātara.

1900. Formation of a separate Irrigation Department. Ceylon contingent sent to South Africa. Boer prisoners of war in Ceylon.

1901. Visit of the Duke of Cornwall and York (King George V.).

1903. Kelani Valley railway opened.

1905. Jaffna connected by rail with Colombo.

1910. Reform of the Legislative Council by the introduction of the elective principle sanctioned.

1911. Rubber a most important factor in Ceylon commerce.

1914. Outbreak of the Great War ; a Ceylon contingent dispatched for service.

INDEX